CW00866370

TONY
WILLIAMS

THE
WAY
LIFE
IS

A Memoir

The Way Life Is
Copyright © 2020 by Tony Williams

Tellwell Talent
www.tellwell.ca

ISBN
978-0-2288-2062-8 (Hardcover)
978-0-2288-2063-5 (Paperback)
978-0-2288-2061-1 (eBook)

Table of Contents

Picture yourself in a boat on a river
With tangerine trees and marmalade skies
Nobody knows...

Lucy in the Sky with Diamonds — The Beatles

For us, there is only the trying...

Four Quartets — TS Eliot

The big adventure is to live.

Clive James

Preface

Nobody knows how our life will turn out. What twists and turns it will take. But we have to keep on trying, to live life as well as we can. It's what keeps us alive.

It is in living that our life becomes an adventure. Living and not really knowing what the future holds, it is just The Way Life Is.

When I started work at the OzCo I realised my colleagues were treating me as an intelligent human, their intellectual and social equal. They were interested in my opinions, and they invited me to join them for lunch and to functions in their homes. I was amazed and loved it. No one had ever done this for me before. I realised that I, too, could do this and it was up to me to make my part in it. They also voiced similar political and social justice views that aligned with mine, which encouraged my feelings of equality and acceptance from them and made me more decisive and confident in accepting and voicing my own views about left-leaning politics and social change. These feelings of acceptance and equality were so different to what I had experienced before. I felt appreciated and valued by these people.

I went to Macquarie University, and I was conditionally enrolled as a non-matriculated student, which meant I had to pass all of Year 1 to obtain a Matriculation and full enrolment status. I wandered around campus in a sort of unknowing daze in the first semester, thinking that here I was almost thirty and surrounded by so many younger people. I didn't know anyone, I had no job, no career, no real relationship [as yet] and I didn't even know how to write an essay! I felt a great sense of achievement when I passed the first year with admirable results.

I was amazed and thrilled. I had a brain! By the end of the four years I had become the first person in my family to finish high school, travel overseas and graduate from university.

The book was written in an attempt to make sense of my life and to look at why and how I have turned out the way I have. I talk about why I made the decisions I did and what the impact of these decisions was. The reader will see how I proceeded from that point and how my life turned out. The text grew out of myriad journal entries written over the last ten to fifteen years. The journalling was an attempt to note the events of the day at the time.

I hope that the major themes shed some light on the impact of these areas on a person's development. I explore themes of marginalisation as a child, of disability, victimization through bullying, loneliness and the lack of parental and educational support, and the impact this had on my development. Overlaying this was the struggle to work through the effects of culturally internalised homophobia and deal with an emerging gay sexuality and its impact on self-acceptance, self-confidence and manhood.

In writing this book I wanted to reach an understanding and an acceptance of what shaped me and how I responded to the events as they unfolded. I look at my contribution to them and the impact they had on me and my development, my life and my relationships. I look at how they contributed to the decisions I made about my life and its directions and to the outcomes that ensued.

It is an attempt to look at the events and relationships that contributed to my sense of self, my self-worth, my concept of myself as a gay man living in Australia at this time, a father, a husband and partner.

It is a search for self-worth through travel, education, parenthood and work to eventually reach a level of self-acceptance and emotional independence that make this examination of the journey rewarding.

It is a journey through a life that has been less ordinary, an eventful life of many challenges.

Chapter One

Nobody Knew

I'll start before I was born because that's when the foundation for my life was laid. It's why whatever happened, happened.

Mackie, my father, was born the fourth son of a family of six; five boys and the youngest a girl. Though I don't know much about his early family life it appears he lived comfortably for the time, in Ryde, a suburb of Sydney. He had a relatively safe upbringing playing with his brothers on the tennis court next door, exploring the creek at the end of the street, and, I hope, experiencing a loving family environment. The youngest, his sister, was Mum's best friend during World War II from 1939-1945.

Mackie's dad was a furniture maker, and it appears he made a good living to support his family between the war years. He died during the war when Mackie was overseas in a Japanese prisoner of war (POW) camp. His mother lived through the war, seeing her sons return from service when so many mothers didn't; some men were more damaged by the experience than others. I only remember an old white-haired lady sitting on a chair in the sun.

As the fourth son in a big family of boys, Mackie appears to have grown into a quiet and respectful young man who was protected from the harsh realities of the wider world. He left school before his Intermediate Certificate, so it appears he was not academically inclined. His family survived the Depression well, and Mackie, then eighteen, enlisted for World War II along with his mates who were all doing it as well. He made it as far as Timor. His battalion was captured by the Japanese, and Mackie spent the next four years or so in POW camps, firstly in Timor, then Java, then Changi and on the infamous Burma Railway. His last stop was near Nagasaki, Japan. He saw the cloud from the atomic bomb that was dropped on Nagasaki, then watched the ash of the cloud and the fires of the burning city settle over the camp. He was among those lined up to be slaughtered by the Japanese when the prison guards simply departed. They left the POWs, weakened by years of brutality and starvation, waiting and wondering whether they would be liberated by the victorious Americans.

He appears to have landed a job as a medical orderly in the POW camp hospital. He would have seen the daily horrors of war and the mistreatment of young men like him. He would have helped the survivors of the death camp; he would have watched them suffer and then die, helpless to do more. The hospital had no drugs and no medical equipment save for basic tools they fashioned themselves. He experienced the trauma of war, the needless death, the brutality with which they were treated, the futility, and the loss of young lives. Yet he survived — physically, at least.

Mackie would have survived in part because he did not directly work on the construction of the Burma Railway, so he would not have been subject to as much of the brutal treatment doled out daily by the guards as they forced the weakened men to march and work. But he was witness to the brutality and helpless to intervene.

I saw a photo I think was him many years ago in a newspaper article. He was a young boy sitting on the end of a camp stretcher in a camp hospital. He looked so vulnerable and trusting. I wish I had sought out that photo and ordered a copy of it. He was looking directly at the camera with big, dark eyes.

Although he survived physically, his emotional and mental health was not so good.

Once liberated, the survivors were taken to camps in the Philippines where they stayed for several months. They were changed in ways no one understood at the time. No one was prepared for the fallout of these young men returning from a brutal war. The time in the Philippines was for "rehabilitation," which meant feeding them so they would not arrive home as emaciated as when they were found. There would have been lots of "the war's over, let's get on with life," but the little help they received was ineffective. There was no emotional support to help these young men and women work through their trauma.

Once home, Mackie couldn't settle. He started a pastry chef course but that didn't last very long. Soon after he arrived home, he met June, his sister's best friend, and they married in 1946. Mackie got a job in the Post Office as a delivery person. Understandably, his children started arriving immediately.

The first child, a son, was born with a cleft palate and harelip; his face was badly deformed. I was that first born.

This would have been a real blow to Mackie who was just back from the trauma of war and starting a new life while trying to forget the past. It must have been a shock and a challenge to both he and June at the start of their life together. Mackie was confronted daily by a deformed first-born. I was a permanent reminder of his trauma, his inadequate ability to deal with the lot he had drawn, and

— what society believed at the time — a testament to a fault in their genetics. This must have been a challenge Mackie was not equipped to overcome. He retreated emotionally from me. Of the many subsequent children Mackie and June had, eight in all, my siblings, none of the others were affected by this deformity.

As the years passed and the children survived into young adulthood it became clear that they were affected in other ways, which was a product of the trauma Mackie brought to their lives. He brought love, too, but his own trauma — what we now know as Post Traumatic Stress Disorder — affected the entire family; it is a generational trauma that affects many descendants of war.

Chapter Two

Mackie's Trauma

As young people, we develop our sense of self, of who we are, through our perceptions of how others respond to us. We observe how we are perceived and the behaviour, love and support (or lack thereof) that important people in our lives give to us. My dad rejected me, but I observed how he supported and interacted with my siblings. Naturally, I compared the acceptance I saw him give with what I received from him: distance, marginalisation, rejection.

I spent my life trying to see past the face in the mirror. I could not hide from the knowledge that it is this face that everyone else also looks at. There is no hiding place. It affected everything I did, everything I thought about; it defined me. This haunted me for many years. It became who I was.

There are others who are far more affected by deformity and handicap than I am, but I saw them receive much more love and support from significant others — and by society as a whole — than I did. My hardship was never discussed, was never recognised, and I was never asked how it was for me.

So, I was confronted daily by my face, the shame and confusion it engendered, the feeling of rejection from my father, and the perceived rejection of others.

I carried the unresolvable shame of "never being good enough."

One incident sticks in my mind from when I was a kid. One day, Dad was going to the paddock to do some fencing. I was standing at the back veranda and hoped he would ask me to come with him. He took my brother Bill by the hand and said he could come with him to the fence. I longed for Dad to ask me, but he didn't. "You stay and help your mother," he said to me. I watched in stunned silence as Bill and Dad left together.

This defined me. My life's role was to be a helper, a supporter. I have played this supportive role my whole life. It became who I was to myself and others.

I experienced a lack of contact from Dad. He avoided me and preferred my siblings. In later years, in many ways I did not blame him and spent many years trying to forgive him, with moderate success. I recognised that he was a victim of his own unresolved trauma and his upbringing in a world where men did not complain and were expected to "get over it and get on with it." Fortunately, we now recognise the effect PTSD has on people who are exposed to life-threatening trauma. Society now tries to do something about it.

Dad coped with his trauma and circumstances by withdrawing and, as he got older, by drinking heavily. As far as I know, he never discussed his war experiences with anyone, not even with Mum or his children. The only person who ever got Mackie to talk was my wife, Maeve. Maeve and Dad would disappear into the lounge room and she could get him to open up but then he would dissolve into tears and sobbing. That was the end of that opportunity to talk. He would clam up again until the next time, perhaps years later. He took a lot of solace in alcohol, which caused unpredictable behaviour. He would be sober for ages then suddenly he would arrive home absolutely raging and we were afraid of what might happen.

He could get violent at the drop of a hat. It seemed that at any time he could react suddenly with irrational anger. We never really knew when he might "blow up" or how he might be with us kids. Alcohol increased the chances of him "losing it," and we all developed an underlying wariness towards Dad. I didn't trust or respect him. I was always aware that he might become reactive and violent. His violent outbursts weren't frequent, just unpredictable. He was often withdrawn and moody. But there was an ever-present wariness about Dad's potential for a violent outburst, especially after a binge.

One outburst occurred on Christmas Day when I was about six or seven. Christmas was always a bit of a fraught time. My parents had very little spare money, lots of kids to buy for, and difficulties allocating what they had available. Dad lost his block about some issue and I was with him when, in a blind rage, he tore the door off the wardrobe in his bedroom and then jumped out the window. I watched him cross the paddock to get away and cool down. I was appalled at his temper but glad he didn't attack me for simply being there (as he had in the past and would do again).

Yet it also seemed that underneath he was a gentle man, lost, quiet, troubled and unhappy with his lot. He seemed confused with what life had dealt him and didn't have the wherewithal to effect positive change in his life or his family. He was the quiet, slight young man in the photo. His war experiences and PTSD along with marriage and the struggle to support the many mouths that kept arriving must have been difficult, confusing and frustrating. He had no education and little money to cope.

I can see now, over sixty years later, how Dad's trauma has been passed down to his children. It remains to be seen if this is passed down to the next generation and the emerging next one to some degree or other. As a parent, grandparent and uncle, I hope not.

I can see how my siblings have been affected and how each of us has adapted and responded to our circumstances. We all found ways to cope. Dad's grandchildren seem to have learned ways to cope as well, some better than others, some extremely well. There are exceptions, but many have gone on to university education and higher degrees, good careers, travel, steady relationships and families of their own.

Mackie's children have, to some degree or other, sought solace in alcohol or drugs, Pentecostal religion or occasional violence. Many have not progressed at school or careers and have all struggled with societal expectations to a degree. We are all good people, as were Mackie and June, but we have been touched by this generational trauma.

I can also see my reactions to the trauma I have experienced. It leads to an inability to respond appropriately or behave in a way that deals with the challenging event in a productive and adult way. I can become "frozen" and unable to respond in a mature way when faced with the unpredictable, confrontational anger of others.

I have managed to overcome my shame to a great degree, though it may never leave me. I am thankful and relieved it has not reappeared in my siblings, my children or in any subsequent generations. Here's hoping it was a one-off in the human gene train.

I have my own theory though, totally unscientific and untested, to explain this phenomenon. Dad was only a few kilometres from the Nagasaki blast. I was conceived less than twenty-four months later and ended up with this blasted cleft palate and harelip. There is no history of this deformity in either side of the family. So, I like to explain it as a product of the nuclear bomb. A product of the inhumanity of war. Touched by the Nagasaki plume.

Chapter Three

My Parents' Family

My early life was spent in Ryde, a suburb to the northwest of Sydney where Dad and Mum had grown up. Mum had gone to the Catholic Girls School in Ryde and got her Intermediate Certificate. She did a secretarial course and worked in a factory office until she met Dad after the war. She was a lively girl who enjoyed wartime Sydney with its visiting sailors and service men in town to relax and have fun on their brief stay. She was a good dancer and enjoyed it. Later when we lived at Stannix Park Road, we used to go to the local monthly Glossodia Women's Association [GWA] dances at the Glossodia Hall. I would dance with Mum, doing the *Canadian Three Step*, the *La Bomba*, the *Pride of Erin* and the *Barn Dance*. I loved dancing, socialising and moving to the music.

Mum was the second daughter of Bert and Ellen. Aunty Margaret, or Peggy as we knew her, was born first, then Mum, Daphne and Paul. Mum was the first to get married and start having a family, Daphne also married straight after the war and had five children. Paul was married a little later (he was seventeen years older than me) and had four children. Aunty Peg never married, and she stayed living in the family home in Ryde, caring for Pop, their father, until he died. Peg died at eighty-eight years old. Eighty-eight years living in the same place.

The house always seemed a bit "spare" and rather soulless, more so after Pop died and it was just Peg living there. You know how a house can reflect the soul of the people who live in it? This house reflected her personality, especially as she got older.

I remember my Grandfather Bert, Pop, very fondly. He was always a gentle man to me, and we would sit on the back step that led up to the garden where he grew vegetables all through the Depression to feed his family. We would talk while he peeled the potatoes for dinner. He would sometimes visit us at Stannix Park, and we would excitedly take him through the bush to our special play spots, trees, creeks and rocks. I wonder if he loved it as much as we loved showing him. I'd like to think he did! Pop was always a stable and supportive presence when we were little.

Pop had been a worker in an "essential industry" during the Depression and grew vegetables for the family, so Mum remembers that they always had food to eat and money for clothes and school if they needed it, unlike many other families during that time.

Bert came from Scotland, and because he is the only grandparent I had, I developed a fond relationship with him up to my teenage years. I have always related more to the Scottish part of my ancestry than with the Irish part.

Although Dad's parents were both Irish, I never knew them. Dad's father died while he was away in the war, his mother lived a few years after I was born but I don't remember much of her except the image of an old grey-haired woman sitting in the sun. I heard from Aunty Peg many years later that Dad's side of the family blamed Mum's family for my facial disfigurement as "it must have come from the mother's side" because it was not evident in the Williams' side of the family. However, it wasn't evident on my mother's side, the Beatons or MacInerneys, either but that doesn't seem to have made any difference to Dad's family. It was an understandable but ignorant view, and we know better now; it would have been hurtful to both Mum and Dad.

I imagine this would have affected their relationship with Dad's family, and it seems we did not see much of them when we were kids, except for Dad's younger sister and her family who used to visit occasionally. I didn't look forward to these visits as it seemed my cousins got yelled at and thrashed with a stick all the time. I really felt for them.

My grandmother, Mum's mother Ellen, was also of Irish descent. I remember her as a grey-haired old woman who was in a hospital. She was placed there when Mum was about eleven years old. Mum took me to see her one day — it seemed like a special occasion as I remember she made a special point of the excursion. I must have been about three or four years old. I have this image of walking through a rather sparse and severe parkland area. There was a curved driveway lined with palm trees, which I always thought were an unfriendly type of tree. I believe this was a part of Callan Park Hospital in Rozelle, Sydney, a mental hospital in those days.

Mum took me into the ward to see this old grey-haired woman in a hospital bed looking at me without much interest. I believe she died a few years after we had moved away from Ryde because Mum went to Sydney for the day for a funeral, which seemed a special event at that time. Later, Mum told me that her mum had been hospitalised when Mum was about eleven, so that would have been when Ellen was in her late 40's or early 50's, as a result of a "breakdown." Maybe it was menopause, maybe it was depression, who knows? I find it amazing that an adult woman with a young family was hospitalised for the rest of her life for what would now be an eminently treatable illness.

Years later I saw some letters to the hospital matron concerning my grandmother. Bert and Aunty Peg had written to send money to Ellen through the hospital administration. I was struck by the really placatory tone of the letters, deferring to the matron of the hospital, and not asserting a right to see Ellen or have contact with her. This was rather amazing. It was dispiriting to sense the powerlessness of the writers and the lack of assertiveness toward the hospital staff in asking for contact or passing on love and concern. They enclosed money for a small gift. I wonder if it was ever used to buy Ellen some small luxury such as perfumed soap or a linen hankie, as they requested. It was too painful for Mum and her sisters to talk about their mother, and when I asked why she was left there for all those years they looked sad and gave non-committal answers.

So, essentially, Mum grew up in a single parent family and Aunty Peg appears to have assumed the running of the home. Aunty Peg was most special to me when I was young. She was the most conservative of the three sisters, the one who stayed behind to look after their father, and the one who worked all her life. She was the "maiden aunt" who never married. When I was feeling neglected by my parents I would fantasise that I was Aunty Peggy's child, but I had to live with Mackie and June because Aunty Peggy wasn't married!

Aunty Peg disapproved of Mackie and thought he wasn't a good provider or a good father. I'm sure she had many other words to describe how she felt about him. She and Mum had words over the years and at times there were periods of no communication when Mum got too impatient and frustrated with her meddling comments and unsolicited advice.

I was Aunty Peg's eldest nephew, and I occupied a special place in her affections because of it. Aunty Peg was good to me, especially in my younger life. I would travel down from Glossodia to stay with her, and she would take me to see musicals and theatre and treat me as special. She exposed me to a world outside of the bush, a world of fantasy, dance and song that opened my eyes. This wonderful introduction to the world of theatre, dance and films meant that in later years I had the confidence to go and see ballet, opera, plays, musicals and theatre shows, art and exhibitions. I've gleaned great enjoyment from this over the years and this early exposure to various art forms encouraged me to pursue my own interests in dance, crafts and painting in later years. It gave me the courage to attend classes and helped me to see if I had enough talent to pursue a career full-time. I don't believe that my younger siblings had this advantage, and it shows in their lack of interest in these forms of entertainment.

Chapter Four

Stannix Park Road and My Immediate Family

In the early years we lived in Ryde in a house on Douglas Street, Putney, a suburb in Ryde near the Parramatta River. Later we moved down the south coast where Dad went to work for a couple of years. When I turned five, I started school at the local Catholic school in Ryde, although only for the last term until that summer because then Dad moved us to Stannix Park Road.

The house at Stannix Park Road was at the end of a dirt track near a swamp. This was a formative time of my life that ignited my love and passion for the Australian bush and its natural beauty, the environment and the wildlife.

Stannix Park Road was as far away as Dad could get from his life up to then. This was forty-seven acres of bush, sandstone and sandy country that Dad tried to farm and make productive. He made this move in an attempt to escape the traumas of the war. It was wild, beautiful mountain and gorge country, which I loved. However, it was not at all suitable for basic farming and supporting a family. Dad succeeded in escaping the city but gave himself and Mum years of laborious and difficult toil while barely meeting the needs of their growing family.

June was his for life, but he appears to have given her little thought when he chose such an isolated spot as Stannix Park Road. There were no modern conveniences except a telephone. The house had no electricity, tanks provided the only water supply, and there were no labour-saving conveniences such as a washing machine or decent stove. Lighting was kerosene wick or mantle lamps or candles, and there was an old Silent Knight kerosene fridge that always threw a nervous collapse on the hottest day of the year. There was no local grocery store or local school. They were miles away from anywhere. Mum had three children under three and was pregnant with the fourth when we moved to Stannix Park Road. She continued bearing his children, eight in all, for years.

I recall travelling out along the Putty Road in Dad's old olive-green Model T Ford. It had deep, wide, roomy bench seats, a running board and a square roof. Mum sat in the front seat with Belle, our black Labrador pup, on her lap. I loved that car because there was so much room for all the kids in the back. There were no seat belts to restrain us then!

One day we were rumbling along the Putty Road headed for home when a back wheel came off. We watched from the back seat as it spun off down the hill in front of us. Meanwhile the old Model T ground to a halt on its rim.

We used to squeeze toward the back of the seat so Dad couldn't reach us if we were making too much noise. He would wave his arm trying to connect with one of us, but we squashed away from him. Once we were going down the big hill yelling at the top of our voices "Over the bridge! Over the bridge! Over the brrrridge!" as we approached it! Dad swished his arm back at us, frustrating for him but safe for us. That was fun and we giggled nervously as we huddled at the back of the seat.

My brothers and sisters seemed to arrive at periodic intervals during our time at Stannix Park Road. Bill, my oldest brother, was much more of a "boy" than I was and seemed to be able to do all the things boys did. He helped Dad, climbed trees, conquered his fear of cicadas, and he could fix bikes and old cars. He was more capable than me, or at least than I felt I was. As we grew older, he became my lifeline to the outside world, the neighbours' kids, the kids we rode with to school, the youth group we joined later, and then the army when we were conscripted. As we got older, I relied on him for friends, I tagged along with him when he went out with his mates from school, and later when we were teenagers. I didn't have the confidence to launch out on my own and it was easier to tag along with Bill and his friends than be at home alone.

My sister Maree was born soon after Bill. She was always a pretty child and seemed to be a favourite among the family. Or so it appeared to me. Maree had her own room off the kitchen because she was the girl, while Bill and I had to share rooms and beds with our younger siblings. I haven't had as easy a relationship with Maree as I have with Bill. He was always fun and mischievous and, apart from the usual sibling rivalry, disagreements, and fights when we were kids, we had and continue to have a good relationship.

Harry was next. He was always a quiet and thoughtful boy who came along with us on our adventures, keeping up and never complaining. I have this image of him clad only in his small shorts, holding a thermometer that showed 110 degrees; an extremely hot day.

Once, we were climbing trees near the stream and our neighbour, Mrs. Anstiss, was with us. Harry climbed to the very top of a young wattle tree that had very thin branches. He was very high and very tiny. As he tried to regain the stalk of the tree, he kept flipping from one side to the other. We all looked on with anxious amusement, but poor Mrs. Anstiss was terrified he would fall. He didn't. Just held on for grim death until he stopped flipping and slowly climbed down again!

Alice was next and was very close in age to Harry. I was the big brother for Alice and looked out for her when she was a toddler. Not that she would remember. In later years I developed a more relaxed and equal relationship with Alice and have enjoyed her support and company over the adult years of our relationship. Alice always tried to be included in our escapades in the bush, but her legs wouldn't keep up. Consequently, it fell to me as the eldest to go back and pick her up and carry her through the bush or pacify her if she was distressed. Later she did the same for me in her campervan. We went on a road trip across the Nullabor Plain. Very flat. But the company was grand. Crossing the Nullabor is a classic Australian journey.

Donny came next when I was about eleven. I remember Mum heavily pregnant getting ready to go to hospital for the birth. A neighbour took her to the hospital in Windsor, as Dad was away at Warragamba Dam where he worked for years. The next day, Dad was admitted to hospital because he was heavily jaundiced with hepatitis. With Mum in hospital with Donny we were at home by ourselves. Jim Larkin, our neighbour, came over, took one look at us and said, "Well you can't stay here so you'd better come and stay at our place." He was a man of few words, so this statement meant he was serious. I don't know what his wife Gloria, Mrs. Larkin, thought of being landed with five additional mouths to feed and find a bed for but she did, and I remember that we were made comfortable and welcome. Mum soon came home, and we visited Dad in hospital. He took a while to recover.

Many years later I had the chance to thank Gloria Larkin for her and Jim's generosity when I gave a eulogy at Jim's funeral. Bill gave me lots of notes to remind me of the positive attributes of Jim and what he meant to us as kids, so that made it easier.

Jack, child number seven, was born when I was in my last year at high school. I felt it was about time Mum stopped having babies. Jack had a difficult time at school and gave Mum some grief with his behaviour, but I think it was more an educational difficulty that Jack exhibited that the teachers were unwilling or incapable of dealing positively with.

Nick, the youngest, was born when I was eighteen years old and out of home. Nick was a very good looking, quiet and thoughtful boy as a child. We could have quite serious and deep conversations about his life and thoughts. He became a wild one, drinking and getting into fights, which created a distance between us. I had trouble understanding why the change had occurred. In fact, all my brothers have had fights over the years and though I feel I get on with them all well now, I still feel a note of caution if they're angry or annoyed.

Chapter Five

Life Was Free

Stannix Park Road was a wild and beautiful place to grow up. The bush and flowers were so diverse. They flourished in the harsh climate of freezing winter nights and grew beautifully in the glorious spring weather and the unbearably hot summer days when temperatures got to over 40 degrees C.

Stannix Park invokes images of a comfortable and well-appointed estate or a property of the well-to-do. Far from it! Stannix Park Road, where we lived in a dilapidated fibro and iron house at the end of a sandy track, was not in any terms an "estate." The actual Stannix Park was an abandoned rock and sandstone house built by convicts at the farther end of Stannix Park Road, farther on than our house. We explored it on our many walking forays as we ventured farther from our house into the wildlands of the swamps, rocky hills and bush.

Night-times in the bush held wonder. I remember standing barefoot on the cement at the back door in the crisp winter night, gazing in awe and amazement at the panoply of stars and planets that stretched across the sky. We watched the progress of the first Russian satellite as it made its lonely way across the arc of the black sky. The stars were so numerous and the depth of the sky so black and crisp; there was no competition from street lights there. It filled me with astonishment then, and even more so now as our knowledge of the amazing universe grows exponentially. Right now, scientists estimate the farthest known universes and stars to be thirteen billion light years away. And the galaxy keeps growing.

One night, Mum called us out of our beds to come outside and see the Aurora Borealis. We stood and gasped in amazement as these curtains of green light rippled and surged above our heads for ages. It was a spectacular and unique sight that I have never forgotten and not seen again.

Dinner was always a busy time. We had to have our "bath" and get ready for bed before Mum served dinner. We wore our hand-me-down pyjamas and gathered around the table waiting for Mum to serve dinner. It was generally a good time. As soon as dinner was served and Mum said grace we dived in. First finished got any leftovers!

Being the eldest I always seemed to finish first and sometimes when I was still hungry I leant over and pinched something off someone else's plate. I'll never forget Alice's look of amazed disappointment when I gobbled something she was saving for last. I got into strife that time and only rarely did it again. I gained a reputation among my younger siblings of being a "garbage guts." Later, when I was working in Sydney and came home for the weekend they would audibly moan "Oh, back to the small meals again!"

Mum was always able to feed us; she was always able to have a meal on the table. Once when she must have been pretty broke, she served us tripe with white sauce. I remember all these expectant little faces around the table in the kitchen waiting for Mum to serve dinner. When the tripe arrived, we just looked at our plates and looked at her. No one touched it. She must have felt terrible. She removed the plates and I don't remember what we did eat on that occasion, but we were never served tripe again.

Dad tried to make this bush, sandstone and sandy country productive over the years. With his attempts to escape the trauma of war this must have been soul destroying for him. Very little he tried seemed to work. We had a couple of head of cattle, and sometimes they would calve so we had calves too. One time we found one of the calves' dead in the paddock. It looked like it had fallen and broken its neck. I felt for Dad as it was a big loss, but it seemed typical of his luck even then.

We had chickens and ducks, too, and often they would perish, or be burnt to death if the kerosene brooder caught fire. The chickens mostly stayed in the chook run so they were protected from foxes. The ducks were allowed to roam around the paddock and graze on the grass. They had a good life. Once I saw a snake weaving through the grass and the duck was watching this strange phenomenon as the snake went past it. The next day we found that duck dead in the grass.

One day, Dad had the front paddock ploughed, which would have cost him a lot of money. He bought about a hundred orange tree saplings, and we spent many hours planting them around the paddock. It looked great; an orchard in the front paddock. That very afternoon a violent storm swept across the swamp, through the big trees on the swamp and hit Dad's newly-ploughed paddock with our newly-planted orchard. We watched, mouths agape, from the house as the huge storm swept through the paddock with such force. Many of the new trees were swept away in the downpour and the paddock eroded from the run-off of the rain.

In addition, Dad hadn't made plans for watering the young trees. Those that remained eventually died of thirst, a great waste of energy, money, labour and most of all, hope. It must have been soul destroying for him as the years passed and his efforts at farming withered and perished.

For all of the years we lived at Stannix Park Road we had an old iron dunny attached to one of the sheds close to the house. One of my jobs as I got older — about ten or eleven — was emptying the toilet can when it was full. I hated it so much I used to put it off until it was actually overflowing. Then no matter if it was overflowing or not, I had to struggle to carry it down below the rocks near the toilet, dig a hole and bury it. That soil became so fertile over the years and later made a very productive vegetable garden. The dunny was always a great hang-out for redback spiders, and when we went to use it we were supposed to check first that there were no redbacks under the seat. There often were and I'm amazed that none of us ever got bitten.

The acres of wilderness provided a marvellous playground of bush and rocks and places to play. The animal and bird life abounded, and we grew up in a unique outdoor utopia that could not be had elsewhere. I still love the rough sandstone hills and bush of the Colo area. A wild, untamed wonderland. It was an awesome array of plants and birds and weather patterns. We observed the birdlife and listened to their calls. We played in the bushes and trees, and we chewed the gum leaves for flavour and when we were thirsty. We smelled the flowers, especially the boronia; it had the most aromatic scent. We sat for hours grinding rocks across the soft sandstone surface, making a scraping hole in the rock and achieving a pile of coloured sand that made a beautiful coloured paste that was good for drawing on our skin. It was something the indigenous people before us used to do to decorate their bodies, and still do.

We developed a love for the bush and the rocks, the flowers and the birds. Spending those hours of quiet time with no one else but ourselves and the birds and the lizards, we developed and absorbed an appreciation of the quietness, beauty and spirit of the bush.

Our house was at the bottom of the track near the creek and above the swamp. It was a decrepit house when we moved in. Dad used poles from the chook yard to prop up the fibro sheeting on the ceiling. There was asbestos fibro everywhere. The whole house was fibro inside and out. It had two bedrooms at the front and then a very roomy living room with a large fireplace at one end. The kitchen and another bedroom (that became my sister's room) were in front of the fireplace, then the back veranda had a bathroom at one end. The laundry adjoined the bathroom. It sounds roomy and grand, but the facilities were pretty old, basic and unstable.

The fireplace was great on winter's nights. We would have a roaring fire that was so hot we had to move back from it. The bathroom had a bath only. Eventually, we got the water heater, which ran on woodchips, going. Before that, we used to get bathed in a bucket in the bath.

The laundry had two tubs and that's all. Mum had a copper tub inside a forty-four-gallon drum with a hole cut below it so the copper tub could be heated. Later, Mum got an old hand-operated washing machine with a hand wringer attachment. That made life a little more efficient for her.

Of the front bedrooms one was Dad and Mum's and I slept in the other for some time. The ceiling had fallen in and there was only a galvanised roof. It was OK in summer but freezing cold in winter.

The kitchen had an old fuel stove that worked for all the years we were there. We always had to collect sticks for the stove, and then later for the chip heater in the bathroom. Mum produced some wonderful meals on that stove.

The back veranda, again fibro, was my bedroom in later years. I built-in the outside wall of the veranda and installed some old louvre windows. It was the first space of my own, and I was proud that I had been able to partition it off by myself for myself.

Even though we moved to the bush at the end of a dirt track near a swamp — as far away as Dad could get from his life — he brought his trauma with him.

Chapter Six

Wild and Beautiful

Life growing up in the bush around Stannix Park Road had its good times. We could roam unhindered through the hills, swamps and creeks and the bush for hours and hours. We had many adventures and scrapes but always found our way safely home again at the end of our wanderings. Being free and allowed to wander and play in the bush for hours was magic. We paddled in a hollowed-out chook egg-layer trough on the creek. We also paddled in a bathtub out over the creek and the swamp when it was in flood. We would be twenty feet up amongst the tall gum trees. We also made tunnels in the banks of the creek like wombat burrows. The walls fell in on Bill once, so we had to drag him out by the legs.

We loved climbing the tall, straight gum-trees beside the house and sticking our heads out the very top, calling to Mum to come out from the house and have a look. "Very good kids," she would say. "Now climb down again." She didn't get mad at us for our foolhardiness, but she would disappear back inside so she didn't have to watch us clamber down.

Dad took us for barbeques into the wild mountain country "up the Colo" and we revelled in the beautiful bush and rock, we walked along tracks for ages and climbed to the top of the steep, rocky hills. It was daring and edgy for us to tip huge rocks off the edge, hearing them crash through the trees down the hill. The Gospers were with us one day and it freaked their parents out well and truly. It certainly wasn't environmentally sound and nor would we do it today, but it was these experiences that helped me and my siblings develop a love of the environment and a passion for protecting it. We could see how it could so easily be ruined or destroyed.

We had to ride our bikes on hot summer days up the dirt track through the bush all the way to school and back again, day after day. We were alone or with the local kids doing the same trip. The striking red-tailed black cockatoos called "arrrkk! arrrkk!" from the bush as we passed.

In summer we could run around all day in only shorts, getting exposed to the heat and the sun without benefit of hat or shirts or sunscreen. We are all paying for that exposure now with aged and weathered skin, moles, skin blemishes and spots, BCCs and sarcomas. Luckily, touch wood, not cancers as yet — but as a result of that carelessness of our younger years the threat is now ever present.

We walked for hours on warm spring days over the hills, around swamps and along creeks, exploring the rocks and the bush. We found abandoned houses on old farms, learned to avoid snakes and goannas, watched the wrens and water birds. We never got lost and would go as far as we liked so long as we were home in time for dinner.

Belle, the pet I grew up with, was a beautiful dog. The gentle, sleek black Labrador was always quiet and reliable. Belle was with us all the time as we wandered through the bush; she was our constant companion. She slept under the house or on the veranda if it was wet, only got the scraps to eat, never complained and always stayed with us kids as we wandered the bush. She was a faithful, loving friend.

When she died, I had to retrieve her body from under the house and I buried her down in the bush. I was fourteen then. I was stricken at the loss, but I guess I saw it as part of the cycle of life. Living on a small battling farm we saw the passing of the seasons, the survival or death of the new calves, the chickens that hatched and survived or wasted and died, and the fruit trees we would labour to plant that withered for lack of water.

Belle's death was my first important loss. I grieved for her and never replaced her in my heart. All the same I saw her death as a part of the cycle of life — how life is — from one stage to the next. Belle's death contributed to my as yet unformed belief that being born and dying are part of a journey all living beings follow.

We spent hours and hours making "drains" through the bush after rain, building dams in the stream and playing in the cool of the trees in the heat of summer.

It took weeks of planning, but we made huge bonfires for cracker night. We stacked up the dead scrub we had cut down. The fires were so fierce and the air around it was so cold. You wanted to get near the warmth, but the fire was so hot you got roasted if you went too near; it was so hot it set the grass ablaze. We had cracker fights on the road with the Simpson kids; it's amazing we survived with eyes and fingers intact.

One hot day, we lit the grassy paddock beside the house and the flames got away on us, so we hid in the bush and watched as Dad beat the flames out. I don't remember if he carried the beating on to us later.

Other memories include my love for sucking the cool water out of the sheets that were hanging on the washing line.

We walked through the heat-stunned bush to the cool creek and swam among the overhanging trees.

We lifted thin layers of ice off the swamp after a freezing night.

We crept up the creek to watch the turtles and the platypus basking on logs in the sun, hearing them plop into the placid water when they sensed we were close.

We caught locusts and tadpoles and green frogs; we were engulfed in the roar of the locusts in the bush on hot summer days.

We picked boronia — its perfume was so beautifully intense.

We watched chickens hatch in the shed and the new babies in bird nests. Dad and Mum used to raise the chickens for food. Bill was able to chop the heads off the chook, but I was too squeamish. Instead, I could hold their legs and Bill would swing the axe. I had a perverse delight in letting the legs go when the head was off and the chicken would do squarking cartwheels across the woodheap spraying blood everywhere.

In the winter afternoons we collected sticks as the cold settled in and snuggled together in front of the fire after our bath. Our bedrooms were so freezing cold that drops of melting icicles fell from the ceiling.

It sounds idyllic. It was — sometimes. Other times it was hard. Freezing in winter we had to get the sticks and the wood for the stove and the fire to warm us or sticks for the water heater to get some warm water. We thought we were lucky to have some warm water in winter.

Chapter Seven

Mum

These were good times, but there were hard times as well. This was especially so for Mum, a suburban girl who enjoyed her youth growing up in Sydney during the war. It must have been hard for her, transplanted to the bush with a seemingly good man who drank and wasn't able to hold a steady job or at least one with some prospects. More and more children kept coming. It sounds like a life of drudgery, but I don't remember Mum ever flagging, complaining or taking to her bed as other mothers might. She was always working to keep us fed, clothed and housed. The only vice she had was the Craven "A" cork tips and she gave those up in her 50s.

She didn't have electricity or the convenient appliances like we have today. She used tank water and hand washed endless dirty clothes in a 44-gallon copper drum.

Some of those years Dad had a job as a timekeeper on Warragamba Dam when it was being built. This meant he was away from home during the shifts he had to work, and Mum was left at home to manage. It was reasonably settled times at home when Dad was away.

Somehow Mum always managed food for dinner and shoes to wear to school, which were things other kids didn't have. Mum was strong, somewhat impatient, firm and fair. She had little time for sympathy and fuss. She was resilient and resourceful, loved her kids and worked hard. She was a good role model for us as we grew and had to find a way to survive in the world.

Another one of my jobs was milking the cow (or cows if two were in milk). Whisky was a beautiful Friesian cow Dad had raised from a calf. She was generally very easy to handle. The other one was Mandy — a flighty red cow who delighted in swishing her tail at my head and, if I wasn't quick enough, stomping her foot into the bucket of warm milk. On winter mornings it was a battle to do the milking but on other days it was a pleasant job to feel the warm milk warming my fingers as it swished into the bucket. If I was milking Whisky, she would be contentedly munching on her chaff. Mandy was more of a challenge because she intentionally swished her tail into my head as I leaned into her while milking.

The cows were always getting out and wandering off, and the fences always needed repair. One day Whisky disappeared, meaning she must have been coming "on heat." Mum asked me to help her find Whisky. It was a beautiful morning and we walked up the creek for hours. As the morning went on I felt hungry and thirsty but didn't want to hassle Mum about that; she would have been feeling the same. As we were walking along the track up the creek, she half-finished one of her Craven "A" cork tips and handed it to me to finish. Although I didn't want to smoke it, I was chuffed that she thought of me as "grown up" enough. Although I had nicked a cigarette or two of hers before, which she had probably noticed was missing, it was like permission to smoke, which I did. I enjoyed it. This experience didn't stand me in good stead later in life when I was living away from home with other young people and I started smoking, as we all did, or seemed to, in those years. To his credit, Bill took one drag of a ciggie when he was about sixteen and hasn't smoked another since. The majority of people in the 60's and 70's seemed to smoke all the time. It's like sunbathing unprotected on the beach when we were young; we are paying the price of sun and smoking now.

My image of myself as a helper and carer evolved. It helped me feel safe. My reason for existing was to help. I became the dutiful son, washing up and helping out without complaint. Setting the table for a meal, cleaning up after dinner, washing up, sweeping the house, bringing the washing in, getting wood for the stove, feeding the chooks, milking the cows, looking after the younger kids and the babies. That was my role.

To get her away from Dad, I used to put Alice in the pram when she was a baby if she wouldn't stop crying. I remember Dad getting angry with her or just generally being irritated, a precursor to losing his temper, and I'd put her in the pram and walk her up the track in the dark until she quieted down and went to sleep. Some nights it was pitch black and I would feel my way up the rough track. I would have been seven years old. Again, I was the helper, but not yet the victim of bullying, the worthless victim. It gave me a role in life. The bullying came soon after.

Chapter Eight

School Should Be Fun for Kids

That first year we were living at Stannix Park Road I was sent to the local Catholic school in Windsor, an eight-mile trip each way by bus in freezing or boiling weather. I must have been in a huge class of kindergarten and infant children. A young Irish nun who wielded a long cane was in charge. One day a harmless blue-tongued lizard crawled quietly along the floor below the blackboard. The young nun freaked out and went into an hysterically berserk rage. She thrashed the poor lizard to shreds in front of all of us kids. I have never forgotten the sight. Subsequently, my sympathies and support have always been with the wildlife, and I have never had any empathy for the Catholic hierarchy.

I only lasted one year at the Catholic school. My parents came to their senses and sent me to the local public school, Glossodia Primary. Bill also started that year. He didn't have a bike so my job was to double him all the way to school and back again along a rough dirt road for most of it. It was bloody hard work.

On my first day at Glossodia Public School, my teacher, Miss Young, asked me what class I was in. As far as I knew I had been in kindergarten at Ryde Catholic School and first class at Windsor Catholic School already. Feeling very important at being asked my opinion I said, pointing at the first row of desks, "Well, I have been in that one, and in that one, so I must be in that one." So, she put me into second class, and I stayed with that group. She would have realised I was too young so at the end of that year I had to repeat second class. However, when the next year started and I was meant to go into third class, the room for the infants' class was too crowded. They promoted me and two of the other "clever" students into the big room in fourth class with the headmaster, Mr. Galverson. That was fine then but in high school I proved to be much too young and it became a real struggle for me to keep up.

I really enjoyed the early years at Glossodia Public School. It was a small school with only eight or ten children in each grade. We all played together at Glossodia Public. I was a reasonably smart kid compared to others, second only to Maggie Penny in my grade. I was a good runner and could hit the ball in rounders. I loved the flavoured milk we got at recess. We had competitions to see who could down a bottle the fastest. The trick was to open your throat and pour it down. I was the hoops champion for keeping one twirling on my neck for fifteen minutes. I had to stop then because the bell went for the end of lunch!

We all rode bikes every day or had to walk to school if the bike was not working, usually because of a puncture or the chain coming off. It was three miles there (about five kilometres) and three miles back. We rode with all the other kids heading our way. We lived in the last house so we had to ride farther than anyone else. Bill started kindergarten the year we all went there, and I had to double him for the first months until he had learned to ride his own bike. I seemed to be always struggling to balance the bike with Bill on it and push us along the road. Bikes didn't have gears in those days.

The day Bill started to ride his own bike couldn't come quick enough as it seemed to me that he sat like a big motionless lump all the way there and all the way back.

Glossodia Public School was a small two teacher school with the infants in the old hall with Ms. Young and the senior classes with Mr. Galverson in the "big" school. Mrs. Galverson taught the girls sewing and was renowned for whacking their knuckles if they made a messy stitch.

After a couple of years at Glossodia, I was fine in the "big" school until I began to be bullied by a kid called Warwick Galverson. Warwick was the son of the headmaster and a year ahead of me. He was bigger and acted with the confidence that comes from his father's position. This was the start of my very unsuccessful school education in the later years of primary school and then all the way through high school.

Warwick delighted in punching me in the stomach, totally winding me just as the bell rang at the end of lunch. Then he'd run into the schoolhouse where his father was in charge, leaving me writhing breathless on the ground to come in after everyone else and be reprimanded by Mr. Galverson for being late. Warwick made my life hell and undermined my confidence at school. I am thankful that he left the year before me and went to high school.

I felt very shamed by being made a fool of in front of the others and unable to defend myself. How could I go to the headmaster for help when he was Warwick's father? I felt helpless and worthless because I couldn't defend myself.

It was here I also first met Viv, whom I'm still friends with. She lived across the road and was about three years old. She used to wander in sometimes and sit at a desk and "write" on some paper the teacher gave her and pretend she was at school with us. Now I hardly ever see her, but we have strongly aligned political views and are always signing each other's political petitions online.

Chapter Nine

High School Trauma

As I was put in the higher grade than my year when at primary school, I was very young when I went to high school, almost twelve months younger than my classmates. I was very physically immature. Since I had been considered intelligent at primary school, and I'd obviously done well, especially in sixth class after Warwick left, I started high school in the "A" class, all the top subjects. All was okay, I was doing well at subjects like Latin, maths, physics and economics until I began to be bullied by a kid called Victor Javik. Victor was a demon to me, and he reawakened the trauma Warwick Galverson had inflicted on me in primary school. In retrospect, Victor Jarvic undermined any chance I had of succeeding at high school and as the years went by damaged my prospects for many years to come.

Victor would seek me out at break and lunch times. He would corner me in the toilet or bubblers shed and belt me into a blithering wreck. I felt totally unable, and I was afraid to resist. Though I hated what Victor was doing to me on an almost daily basis, I felt sorry for him. He was a sad kid who was the son of migrants and had a violent father. But he used me as a punching bag to take out his frustration. He hassled me, followed me and thumped me as often as possible. He was smart; he'd only hit me in the ribs and the stomach or back, not on my face where it could be seen. He made my life totally miserable. There was nowhere to hide and no one to turn to. Again, I was afraid. I felt powerless to resist and stand up for myself and worthless because I didn't resist and couldn't protect myself or assert myself.

High school was pretty much misery for me. My grades suffered because I was too distracted to concentrate and wasn't able to catch on to the lessons. By the end of the first year of high school, I was failing my subjects. In the second year of high school I was put in the "B" grade. I was slipping badly in all my subjects. At sport I was unable, unwilling and incapable of playing or participating in the activities or in team games. I was the one chosen last when picking teams. I didn't seem to be good at any sport, and I got yelled at in frustration by teachers trying to get me to join in. In the end I hated sport and was unwilling to try out for anything because I knew I wouldn't be any good. Again, my response to the trauma of Victor's constant bullying and the teacher's anger and frustration was to shut down, to became defenceless and not be able to stand up for myself or retaliate to protect myself.

I was further traumatised by how some of the teachers perceived my incompetence. No one at the school came to my aid, offered compassion, support or advice or helped me cope in any way. I felt so alone all through high school.

I was obviously depressed, anxious and unsure of myself. My pain must have been obvious. There was no support, no adult anywhere, in fact. I did not feel I could seek support from my parents as I imagined they would tell me to assert myself, and I didn't feel capable of that. I felt useless and marginalised.

This pervasive sense of fear and worthlessness was a huge influence on my inability to stand up for myself.

Looking back, it was a product of being rejected by Dad, ashamed of my facial disfiguration and feeling that I was not worth defending. I felt I somehow deserved this treatment.

I found myself gravitating to the helping role where I felt protected — like at home, with friends, with "the girls" and with teachers. Why did I always do chores, help the teacher clear up, or tidy after a party? It was where I found a role and felt recognised and safe.

The incident where Dad told me to "stay and help your mother" rang in my ears for years. Dad defined my role as "Mother's Helper." I knew I was getting more and more depressed. By the end of Fifth Year, the last year of high school, I barely passed four subjects in the final, the Leaving Certificate, which meant I didn't graduate or qualify for any further study.

This bullying had an ongoing effect on my self-confidence and education for years. It shows what a negative impact bullying during the school years can have on vulnerable individuals. Schools are much more aware of bullying now and have programs to work with bullies and victims, but this is also a story of what can happen if schools and teachers are not diligent and consistent in their support of victims.

Chapter Ten

There's a Difference

I felt different from other kids, and this included feeling an attachment to the wild and beautiful bush I was familiar with, which allowed me to experience the sensations of my emerging sexuality.

I didn't like wrestling with other kids much because it made me feel vulnerable and uneasy. One lunchtime at Glossodia Public I was in a wrestle with a kid called Les. I have this image of him and the feeling of him sitting astride me and holding me down. I didn't want to struggle, just enjoy the pleasant sensation of being held down by another male. I looked up at him astride my chest framed by the blue sky. I felt quite calm, which was a notable and unusual sensation; it was a momentarily serene and welcome experience that I both sought and experienced many times as I wandered alone through the bush.

I found that serenity and solace in the bush. It enabled me to enjoy my sensation of difference and my sexuality. I did love the country that I grew up in and still do. I loved the rocks, the steep hills, the gum-trees and wildflowers, the sandy creeks and swamps, the birdlife of all descriptions, the goannas and the wombats, the huge boulders that terraced up the hills. Beautiful wild country. It made me feel peaceful and safe, and it played into my emerging sexuality.

This country was wildly beautiful and quiet. I loved finding a hidden spot beside a boulder, on a hillside, in a tree, or just lying underneath the scrubby bushes and sitting or lying for what seemed like hours. Not moving, I felt the air, the breezes, watched the clouds and gazed at the blueness of the sky, hearing and seeing the birds and wildlife. It was an escape, my own world, unthreatening and mine to savour and enjoy.

I also felt at times intensely sad and lonely especially as teenage years encroached, and I had few friends I felt close to. I sought quietness and safety in the bush. I enjoyed what the bush had to offer, but I felt this vague, pervasive thought of "Is this all there is?" I felt I did not "fit in" and the constant bullying made it worse. Of course, many adolescents are bullied to one degree or another, but I felt that even then, though I wanted to be a "typical" boy like all the others, I still felt different. I had no idea what it meant, only that I didn't seem to feel like other boys did.

Sometimes I would wander around the bush all day, lost in my thoughts enjoying being with myself. I could explore for ages without seeing another person and only return home when I was hungry or it was getting dark. Mum never set a time when we were expected to return, never said "Don't go too far." I loved exploring and enjoying myself, but I also knew I was escaping from the house and avoiding what that meant. I was also running away from myself and searching for some meaning or belonging.

At one time my brothers and I made a track through the bush below the dam that ran down to the stream at the far side of the block we lived on. We called it the Kokoda Trail. One day when I was about fourteen I walked down there alone. It was a beautiful warm day. I took off my clothes and lay naked on a fallen log in the sun. I wanted someone to find me and caress me, touch me, stroke my skin, make love to me, assure me that I was okay. Not that I knew what that was. I just had this yearning, this longing. I wanted a friend.

I was also growing more attached to the energy and spirit of the land. I understand that our indigenous people have a history of attachment to the land that goes back tens of thousands of years, which I think is simply awe inspiring. But I also felt a strong spiritual attachment, a strong energy of the land and the place I grew up, that I enjoyed wandering through. I don't claim it was anything like the spiritual attachment and energy that indigenous people experience and have, and that the white people have dishonoured, but there is a strong energy there nevertheless.

I loved the statuesque eucalypt gum-trees and still do. There were forests of eucalypts on the hills and gullies around the ridges of the Colo wilderness. We had the most beautiful stand of eucalypts growing near the house at Stannix Park Road. They grew especially tall on the swamp, and when the swamp flooded, we could paddle around the crowns of the trees in our makeshift canoes. I really respond to the energy of these magnificent trees, and it is sad to witness the loss of vegetation and wildlife habitat through the constant clearing of these striking forests.

This exposure to the wild beauty of the areas around Stannix Park Road and the Colo Wilderness engendered in me what I believe to be a spiritual attachment and love of the Australian bush.

Chapter Eleven

The End of High School

As I progressed through my high school years, that pervasive feeling of being different, of longing, increased; in retrospect, these were simply the yearnings of youth. The difference for me was I wasn't yearning for what I was supposed to yearn for. At high school by the end of the first year, I wasn't coping with the level of work, nor did not feel like I was part of any real friendship group. I was being bullied continuously by Victor Jarvic. Sure, I had "friends," but I still felt this separateness, this not belonging, this not being accepted or this feeling of rejection. In retrospect, I was dealing with the trauma of being bullied and this trauma conflicted with the demands of the curriculum and my educational and psychological well-being.

During school I don't remember any worthwhile information about what was available after school, what we could do to improve our chances or explore career options. I had a "vocational interview" at one stage. I indicated on the form that I was interested in "land valuation" and the results came back for me that I was suitable to be a "land valuer." That didn't tell me any information about being a land valuer or what I needed to qualify as one or even about "valuing land," what a land valuer did. Seemed pretty obvious to me that the careers counsellor had just put in "land valuer" as that was what I had indicated so that must mean I'd like that career and that I could qualify as one.

By the end of high school, the end of Year Five after twelve years of school, I was failing at everything and was very unhappy. I had no enthusiasm for school, was still being bullied. I felt anxious, sad and depressed.

At the exams for the Leaving Certificate I felt completely overwhelmed. I didn't feel I was able to effectively answer anything and the exams filled me with terror. I knew I was failing dramatically but felt so powerless to do anything about it. At the end of an exam my fellow students compared notes and shared answers. I just wanted to crawl away and hide.

When the results came out, I had passed four subjects, but that meant I had not passed the Leaving Certificate or Matriculated. I had not qualified for any further study. My Leaving Certificate results certainly didn't indicate that I would get anywhere near qualifying for the Valuation course. I had failed.

I felt helpless to affect change. And what change would I affect anyway? I lived in a limited and small world. I didn't know what was possible. And there was no one, no friend to give me guidance or support. I had failed myself, failed my parents.

After school finished, Dad got me an interview at the local bank where he knew the manager, and I got a job immediately. At least that seemed like a start, but soon I loathed it. It was relentlessly boring counting cheques and entering ledgers. Is this what work life is about? I hated it. I felt even more depressed and ungrateful to my parents and the bank manager for giving me the job. I simply did not know what to do.

After a few months of this mind-numbingly boring work I had a total breakdown. I sat sobbing uncontrollably in the back of Mum's car while she sat in the front. I felt so stupid, so alone and worthless. Hopeless. Why couldn't I help myself like others seemed to do? Why was I making things so hard for Mum and for myself? She couldn't help. Mum was unresponsive in the front seat and never tried to give me any comfort. She didn't ask me what was wrong. Any answer I gave would have left her feeling even more helpless to assist me. I guess she must have felt helpless or she may have despaired that her eldest child was a blubbering wreck. But what were the alternatives? I had no idea and no one offered any suggestions. I was conscious of the fact that Mum had many other kids to deal with as well, and I was the eldest and should be able to look after myself. Why couldn't I? Why was I so hopeless? Why did I feel so helpless?

Mum and Dad talked to me about my going back to school to complete the Leaving Certificate again but by then it was already halfway through the year, and I knew that would not work. I sat for the NSW public service exam and wonder of wonders was accepted into a clerk's job in the city. Great; an escape from the bank, from home.

This meant I had to live in a Catholic Hostel for Working Boys in the inner west. You would imagine it was a great move for a boy from the bush, but I was soon so homesick and unhappy I would catch the train home every weekend because I couldn't bear to be away from the familiarity of my family. Meanwhile, I was so disappointed with myself that I couldn't stay in the city and enjoy it like all the other young country lads I knew at the hostel. It was a very unhappy, lonely and insecure period. Mind you I also didn't have much spare money to be going out. This lack of money fuelled another of my ongoing anxieties: never having enough money.

I wanted to be like others, have a worthwhile job, or be going to technical college to get some qualification.

I wanted to be "normal" like other boys, date girls like other boys did, kiss and cuddle with them. I even tried it, but I'd get to a certain point and then, well, I really didn't want to be doing it. I wasn't interested. Why wasn't I interested? What do I do? It didn't feel comfortable for me. I couldn't work out why it didn't feel right. In a short while I found that keeping busy at work or getting so drunk I could pass out were good avoidance tactics.

Chapter Twelve

A New Life in Sydney

In mid-1964 just before my seventeenth birthday I was living and working in Sydney. Being in the city during the day was great. I felt like I belonged, and I was comfortable. I loved the crowds and the traffic and the busy-ness of it all. I could get lost in all the people and still feel safe.

I worked in an office building in Phillip Street, right in the Central Business District (CBD). There was a lunch take-away downstairs in the arcade that had a great array of cakes and pastries that I had to sample for every morning tea. I could go window shopping at lunchtime, explore the department stores and the arcades, look at the people and enjoy the buzz.

I wished I had a lot of money so I could buy all the appealing clothes the stores tempted me with. I had very little money left over for clothes. I opened an account at Lowes so that I could get reasonable clothes without forking out the money. But Lowes fashion didn't suit me so here I was stuck with a credit account I couldn't afford and the only way I could get new clothes was to put them on the account! With a struggle I did eventually pay the account off and was then able to buy clothes with more appealing style from other shops. This was a good lesson in the use of credit, and it wasn't until much after that I dabbled in credit again.

However, eventually I was able to afford a smart three-piece suit and ties so that I could look like the others. All the young clerks wore suits to work, and I had enough money for new shirts and ties, lunches and beers on Friday nights. I worked in a small group of colleagues all around my age so we chatted and joked and enjoyed working together. I enjoyed the short time I had working with these young people.

There was a girl in our group called Monica who seemed to take a shine to me, although I think she flirted with all the other boys too. She had a boyfriend at home she was always talking about, so I guess this gave her the permission to safely flirt with the guys in our section. It was the time of miniskirts and she delighted in wearing her uniform as short as possible. I had never seen anyone like Monica and enjoyed flirting with her in return. You could see her underwear as she walked around the section. She flirted with me and taught me how to wink! She joked and laughed, and I really enjoyed the attention. I also met David, a chap in our section whom I would later go travelling with.

I loved meeting up with friends — mostly school mates of my brother Bill's and their friends. Friday after work we used to go down to the Rocks to listen to jazz, drink lots of beer to get pissed and have a good time. Once I won a frozen chook in a raffle early in the night. A couple of hours later, we drunkenly kicked it around the bar of the next hotel up George Street.

At the end of my first year working in the city, the Beatles came to Sydney. I had a couple of their records and enough money for a ticket to the old Rushcutters Bay Stadium. I went with a friend from work. We sat in the bleachers in our dapper suits and everyone clapped politely at the end of each song. I heard every word and

I loved it!! I had found something that I could relate to and I could enjoy. I didn't need anyone else for me to have a good time.

At the end of the concert I knew I would love to see them again. They had a sixth concert on Saturday night so, remarkably, I was able to buy two tickets — one for me and one for Maree, my sister — in the bleachers. So, Saturday night Maree and I made the trek all the way from Stannix Park Road to Rushcutters Bay. What a difference two days made. This concert was the complete opposite of the first concert. Everyone went wild and screamed at every song, and I joined in with gusto! You could not hear a word of what was sung! I was delirious with pleasure and screamed along with the best of them.

I came out on cloud nine and we made our long way home floating with pleasure. That concert changed my experience of pop and rock. What a difference it was to leave a Beatles concert in Rushcutters Bay and arrive home to the old house in the bush. That night changed my life because it opened my mind to music, both classical and modern, and the power it has to change our lives.

When I could afford tickets, I loved going to concerts. I am proud to say that I have seen the Beatles live — twice!! I still love their music. The words are so evocative. I'm a lifetime fan.

Chapter Thirteen

Trying to Find Myself

Being close to a Technical and Further Education College (TAFE) meant I was also able to do courses at night. After a few false starts, one of which was failing a maths course that would have helped me get into the land valuation course, I was able to pull things together.

I stuck at it and finally completed a four year, two-nights-a-week certificate course in personnel management at Sydney TAFE. It was a real grind, but interesting; I understood it and passed the exams. It meant I had an education but, more importantly, I proved to myself that I had some ability. Knowing I had some intelligence and meeting people my own age who had travelled already, gave me the urge to travel. It also meant I could get away from the pressures of not knowing what or who I was.

My aim was to start with London as so many were doing then. I was determined to get out of Australia and see what the world was like outside of my small experience. I wanted to change my lonely life. I knew, or hoped it would, help me avoid worrying about my sexuality. The problem was, conscription had been introduced in Australia to support the Australian presence in Vietnam. I had to register for the "call-up," and I was conscripted. I was in the Citizen Military Forces so I wasn't able to travel or leave the country in any case. I ached to get out of the Services. I felt so trapped at this time.

I shared a room with three others at the Hostel for Working Boys. There were about thirty-five young men there, a varied bunch. The matron who ran the place was a bit of a tyrant and had her favourites. I wasn't one of them for some reason. One day she was displeased with the boys and came into our room brandishing a rolled-up *Herald* newspaper. She came over to me and started belting me around the head with it. I was appalled at being treated like this and got out of her way. She was very moody with me after that. I didn't know why. Perhaps it was because I had masturbated onto the sheets? I thought I had been careful to not let that happen. I felt I was again being victimised by someone who should be more caring toward me or at least leave me alone.

One night lots of the boys were engaging in some rowdy behaviour so we went upstairs to check it out. One of the boys upstairs who I thought was handsome had his legs over his head and someone was lighting his farts. I'd never seen fart lighting before and it was quite a sight, this great ball of fire being emitted from his anus. Eventually he ran out of air to push out his arse and got his underpants smouldering for good measure. Hilarious!

They were good blokes, but I never felt really close to any of them. I was afraid they would think I was a sissy, gay or effeminate. I was always fearful of being bullied or criticised. What would I do if I got "hit on"? I should welcome that, but I didn't know how to react if it did happen. I'd retreat into my shell and become pathetic.

One night I came home late by bus after a visit to Aunty Peg's at Ryde. Walking down the street I was accosted by a man who dragged me into a lane and pushed me hard against a fence and held me. I was terrified and he knew it. He kept wanting to know if I'd like to "shove it up hard." I vaguely knew what he meant but the very thought of it was terrifying and I was so afraid I couldn't have managed anything like that in any case! I guess he knew I was a lost cause as eventually he let me go. I ran all the way home to the hostel and dived into bed.

One of my roommates saw this and wanted to know what was the matter with me. I stammered out what had happened. He immediately went to where I had said this took place. I couldn't imagine why until later it dawned on me that it was perhaps to find this man and offer what I couldn't manage. When he came back the room was in darkness and he stood over my bed and wanted to get into bed with me. At least he asked!

I was so shaken by the events of the evening. I was also so afraid of my response to this. If this was what I wanted why was I so timid in my response to this opportunity? I know now that it was a response to further trauma but at this time it just left me more shaken, confused and timidly anxious. I was more unsure of how I wanted to live my life.

After a couple of years at the hostel, I bought a car, and so I got kicked out because the rule was that boys who had a car couldn't live there. I moved home and commuted every day from Stannix Park Road to Windsor by car, from Windsor to Sydney by the old red rattler steam trains and home again in the evening. I enjoyed that time; each day was full and busy and left no time to ponder the meaning of life. A group of us met on the train every morning and afternoon, played cards and smoked our heads off. Unbelievable now; I hate the very smell of smoking.

Work was pretty boring as a junior clerk in the public service, way before the IT age. Everything had to be noted by hand or typewriter. My, how things have changed.

I was living at home, so I had time to fill in at weekends. I looked up to my younger brother Bill and clung to him because he was everything I wasn't; he seemed confident, had friends to socialise with, a bundle of energy and at times he was hilarious. He and I joined the local branch of the Junior Farmers (or later, Rural Youth) for something to do and people to socialise with. I enjoyed the "projects" we had raising chickens or a calf. Bill had a piglet that grew into this huge pig that seemed intelligent; it seemed to pay attention to you when you talked to it. Meeting that intelligent pig formed my decision to stop eating pork.

We occasionally had a weekend away visiting other farms and bunked down with other members. Even then I was terrified that I would be "outed." I was living in such an uptight state of apprehension. Once, I was sharing a bed with a neighbour of ours and during the night I inadvertently touched his body. I became so alert I couldn't sleep, terrified that I would be seen as "not straight," whatever that meant.

At one stage, at the urging of a rather zealous Catholic neighbour, I joined the "Cursistas," a male-only religious group who met, prayed together, and went on retreats where we listened to each other give religious-based talks. I had to give one once and it was so difficult. I was so anxious, and I knew it wasn't me. I didn't feel more loved, wanted or accepting of myself or religion. Finally, I moved away and dropped it. This attempt to find support through religion brought me more shame and confusion rather than peace and self-acceptance, so it was a relief to quit.

I decided to drop religion, to stop trying to be celibate and then to start having sex with women (of course it was women, I wanted to be "normal"). Women or not it was sex and the first positive step I took to rid myself of the guilt and shame I felt around my sexuality. Over the following years I got rid of this Catholic shame, this idiocy around sex and sinning and living by "God's word." What I saw happening in the church was so hypocritical that I felt this view was justified. Another great relief.

As a teenager I used to go to mass every Sunday at Mum's urging and sit there listening to the parish priest extol the virtues of abstinence and the dire consequences of fornication and masturbation. Then I discovered that he had a mistress living around the corner and a fourteen-year-old son. This was the end of my idealistic Catholicism and the realisation that if the priest could be only human, with human foibles and needs, then so was I.

We spent weekends drinking and partying with various friends. I was driving down from Stannix Park Road on weekends to spend it with friends in Darlinghurst. One lot of guys we knew lived in a flat behind the shops in Oxford Street just up from the old Albury Hotel. We used to meet in the bar of the Albury and spend hours on a weekend drinking and smoking there. One Saturday night they were having a party, so we gathered during the day to start grooving. A group of us climbed out on the shop awning over Oxford Street and spent hours there drinking, getting stoned on dope and watching the traffic roll past. It was a fun time and a good way for me to be distracted from my feelings of loneliness and separation. Fuelled by alcohol and grass, I was able to avoid what I knew was inevitable but had no idea how I would get the courage to move myself to that acceptance.

Chapter Fourteen

Conscription and Politics

Bill and I decided to join the local Citizens Military Forces (CMF) Unit. I was nineteen, Bill eighteen. It was the time of Australia's involvement in the Vietnam War; Australia was the United States' subservient puppy and Australia's right-wing leaders would do anything for the US master.

It was a good move at first; I swallowed the line of "Make a man of me" though I soon realised how wrong I had been to join up. I had great difficulty coping with the drill sergeant screaming abuse as we were expected to march mindlessly on parade and have our kit polished to perfection every week. We had to repeat this every second weekend and for a two-week camp once a year. The sergeant seemed to single me out for additional abuse and shaming. Again, I had landed myself in a position where I regretted my enlisting almost from the beginning. He was another bully who honed in on me, his victim.

The conservative politicians of Australia introduced conscription in the 1960's and we had to register for the call-up. I remember ticking a box that said that if my number came up, I could elect to serve six years in the CMF as I was already a member. My understanding was that if I wasn't called up, I could leave after the stated two years; but much to my misery this wasn't how it turned out. I was notified that I was called up. I don't know if my name or birthdate actually did go into the ballot or I was automatically called up because I was already in the CMF. Whatever the reason, I was condemned to the army for six years. I certainly didn't want to go to Vietnam in any case. I was opposed to the war even then. As I was called up, I had to spend the next five-and-a-half years in the CMF. I felt trapped and frustrated by these years.

This was the late 60's and early 70's, a time of parties, long hair, smoking dope, opposition to the war in Vietnam, opposition to conscription. It was a time when those in the army were defamed by the opposition to the war. I felt this so keenly. I became vehemently opposed to the war in Vietnam, Australia's role in the massacres of the Vietnamese people and Australia's subservience to the US, yet here I was trapped in the army. It was how I became politicised against military interventions, violence, right-wing politics and media commentators, bullying by superiors in the army and the unquestioned adherence to authority. I hated to comply with the system.

This was a politically formative time for me, Bill and many others. In a way I have this experience to thank for the opposition I still have to authority, the militarisation of the police and the introduction and intervention of "Border Force," a hideous militaristic concept in Australia. I became keenly aware of political self-interest, social justice, the need for equality and benefit for all. I learned about governments that allow the rape of the environment for financial gain for the few, self-interest in all its guises, and the loss of compassion for those escaping war and oppression. Australia's treatment of refugees was and is now reprehensible and in no way reflects an Australian trait of a "fair go."

My opposition to all things military is where my small attempts at subversion were also born. In the army we tried to disguise our long hair by oiling it and putting it up under our beret, but the sergeant got wise to that. We were disciplined, screamed at, made to do onerous duties, bullied, ridiculed and belittled in front of others. Although this was agony for me, I tried to find the means to appear to comply and thus save myself from this constant abuse. I knew it would be easier if I did comply, but I couldn't do what was required of me. I was so strongly opposed to what I was expected to do.

Once, we were servicing the trucks to drive them in convoy for several hours. I inadvertently filled the sump up with water instead of oil, partly by accident and not paying any care or attention to what I was doing, but I was secretly gleeful when I realised what I had done. I drove the truck to its destination. I would guess that the works would have been stuffed after that; well, I hope they were.

At rifle practice we had to achieve a minimum score of hits to pass the proficiency test. I repeatedly shot into the bunker below the targets, and the frustrated abuse of the corporal and sergeant was frightening but perversely satisfying. The small attempts at subversion continued, but I realised they also caused me to be in disfavour with the sergeants.

Though I hated the regimentation and hierarchy of the CMF I enjoyed the camps, bivouacs and marches we went on as part of the training. It got us out into the bush, in the trees and birdlife, the wilds of the Australian bush. I loved that part; I was fit and could keep up, and the regimentation was not as rigorous when we were bivouacking in the bush. Walking through the bush as an adult still gave me a chance to daydream about being enveloped in it when I was a kid.

When I look back on all those years of being bullied, failing at my school work, living away from home in the city, trying to study at night, not feeling like I had any luck with being like other young men my age, I realise how depressed and anxious I was. I felt so alone all the time. It was before the time of it being okay to see a psychologist or a counsellor or even before they existed. I wouldn't have had the money, but at least being able to talk to someone about my anxieties and depression may have helped. The world has progressed so much in this area and youth mental health is a much talked about issue these days.

Chapter Fifteen

Family First

In the late sixties and early seventies, Bill, Maree and I had moved back to Sydney from Stannix Park Road. We had jobs in the city by this time, so life was centred there. I was sharing a tiny flat at Coogee Beach with Ben and I in one room and two other friends in the second bedroom. Bill was sharing a flat at Rose Bay with mates. Maree had a flat at Ashfield. We were working, studying at TAFE and partying as much as young people can afford.

At Coogee I was able to spend my time at the beach, slathering myself with coconut oil and sunbaking all day at the weekends, hoping to tan my pale skin. I wanted a body like those I saw at the beach; fit and tanned. I sought the tan but only succeeded in burning myself to a crisp numerous times; my skin would be burnt red and then peel, leaving me as white as before. Like many Australians from Celtic ancestry, I have ongoing trouble with skin lesions and carcinomas, and am still as pale as ever. I know these endless hours hiding at the beach were another way of me avoiding myself and hoping that I would change, but it also came with consequences for my skin.

However, life was good with parties on the weekend and a large group of friends all living around the inner suburbs.

It was a good distraction for me from the loneliness I felt. We were working and earning, so we had a good time, parties, camping trips, beach holidays, dinners.

One Christmas, a huge group of us went to the annual Christmas ball of one of the group. It was a big and popular event where we dressed up, partied, danced, got drunk and had a great time. Maree, who was a very attractive twenty-year-old, was noticed by a member of the rock band playing the music we danced to all night. Sometime after that party she suddenly disappeared, and we heard later from Dad and Mum that she had turned up in Queensland. We found out the reason — she was pregnant. It must have been a rotten time for her, and as families are, we never got to talk about it. Dad followed her up there and brought her back to Sydney.

Dad and Mum still had a number of our younger siblings at home and did not want a pregnant daughter as well. Bill and I agreed that she could share our flat at Coogee. Our flatmates, to their credit, obliged and moved to the flat at Rose Bay or other accommodation. We found out years later that once Maree was installed at Coogee, Dad and Mum went to Manly to see the father of the child, Jason, and informed him that Maree would be having a termination. They said that if he came anywhere near Maree or tried to contact her Dad would shoot him. I'm sure Dad meant it at the time and Jason, a young muso of the time having a ball, must have really had the wind put up him. We had no further contact with young Jason.

Sometime later, maybe a couple of years, we heard, or were told that Jason had been shot and died in what we assumed was a drug stuff-up. I guess we decided that we weren't surprised at this news and forgot about him. As far as we were concerned that was the end of him. In retrospect maybe that was Dad putting Maree, Bill and I off the scent.

The three of us lived together in Coogee until the birth of Maree's child. Bill and I cared for Maree for those months of the pregnancy, supporting and caring for her, coming home to spend evenings with her. It must have been a boring time for her to sit at home all day by herself. When it was time, we took her to Crown Street Women's Hospital and visited after the birth. The child, a girl Maree named Chrysstina, was adopted soon after the birth, as babies to unwed mothers were in those days. It all seemed harsh and uncaring and perfunctory at the time, but that was how families dealt with unwanted pregnancies to unwed daughters. It happened many thousands of times to young women, as we now know.

Bill, Alice and I felt an attachment to this child we would never know. It was another "secret" that was not discussed but carried close to our hearts. Knowing that a child of the family is adrift somewhere out there left a distant ache.

Maree went home to live with Mackie and June and our younger siblings just before her twenty-first birthday. Soon after she married a local yokel and settled down in the area. She did, however, refuse to have any more children for, as she said, "I lost one, had her taken away. I don't want to lose another." That decision has lain heavily on Maree and on her brothers and sister who knew or have found out about this episode over the years, but Maree has remained steadfast to her decision. Her husband also had to bear Maree's decision.

We thought that episode was over, but for decades we still carried an empty place in our hearts for Chrysstina, our "lost baby." We yearned to find her and bring her back to the family.

Chapter Sixteen

Living in the 70's

By the early 1970's, jobs took Bill and I back to flatting in Sydney. We were still in the CMF and we transferred to a transport regiment in the Eastern Suburbs. I had learned to drive trucks in the CMF and got my Heavy Vehicle driver's licence. I still renew it every year, but I have never used it since leaving the army.

I was sharing a house with young men I had met while living at the hostel. We would have a party, usually on the weekend when we were all off work. We would clean the house and decorate it with streamers and posters and candles all around. We put cellophane paper over the lights so the whole house looked like a somewhat scrappy but fun nightclub and encouraged our friends to dress up in clothes and gear we all bought from op-shops. We filled our house with friends and colleagues in party mode, with loud music, dancing, drugs and raucous good times. By midnight the entire party was out in the backyard or dancing inside, talking, laughing and oblivious to the neighbours. The neighbours were very tolerant as the police only came once when the noise was intolerable. They left after we turned the music down.

At one time we sheltered a young man who had deserted from the US army while in Australia on leave.

He lived with us for many months unable to be seen or to move. He came from a middle-class family in the eastern states. He was a quiet guy and really kept very much to himself, and I didn't get to know him at all. However, it was a good thing for us to do at the time. It was little subversive efforts like this to undermine the war machine that gave some perverse relief and helped me maintain my self-respect as an individual able to act independently.

I look back on the whole Vietnam and army experience as another very tedious and unfortunate experience for me. Later, many men that did national service would say how much they benefitted from it, what a great experience it was for them, yet Australia's treatment of the Vietnam veterans is a shameful part of our history, and I am thankful I am not one of them. I can only say that I hated it from start to finish, and I worked to support any opposition to the war machine that I could reasonably do. I was determined to stay out of detention, the threat of which frightened me to bits. These years helped me consolidate the skills of resilience, of political activism and left-wing politics.

The latter years of the Vietnam War up to 1972 were marked by increasing opposition to the war through rallies and the increasing violence of the right-wing state forces in opposing the rallies. Even though we had the fear that the authorities could arrest us or report us we still tried to show our opposition any way we could.

Gough Whitlam, at that time head of the left-wing Labour Party, was elected as Prime Minister in 1972. He certainly changed the opportunities available to me and consequently the direction of my life. He implemented a wonderful agenda of social and social justice change. He enabled me to free myself of the Armed Forces, opened up tertiary education and made it free, and introduced the concept of Mature Age Students. He revitalised the public health system and was instrumental in implementing many other socially beneficial reforms that improved the standard and quality of my life.

It is unfortunate that over the intervening years many of the reforms introduced by Whitlam were changed and watered down so that the original purpose was lost. Whitlam implemented many changes in the areas of social justice, domestic reforms and indigenous acceptance. His time in office also changed the way many Australians think and respond to issues such as equality of minorities including gays and women, the treatment of refugees, providing adequate welfare and assistance for the unemployed, the indigenous people, the homeless and refugees. Whitlam also changed the way the public service operates and provides facilities and introduced changes in education, health and environmental benefits. Many of these have been decimated, privatised and in many ways changed for the worse by subsequent governments — mostly, but not all, from the conservative side of politics. Overall though, the Whitlam years and his legacy of social and political change have indeed challenged and changed the political face of Australia in many ways.

Chapter Seventeen

Still Searching

By the early seventies, work was largely unfulfilling and tedious, but it was a means to an end. I earned just enough money to pay rent with a little left over to get ripped on the weekends. These elements helped me avoid the pain and confusion of not having a girlfriend and the fear of what I was expected to do. I watched my mates slip easily into having a regular hetero relationship. I was lonely so I drank, which gave me the excuse to avoid other pressures.

I was very depressed, unhappy, withdrawn and sad during this time. I tried getting back into religion until I knew it was stuffing me up more than I was already. I tried to conform to the tenets of Catholicism and only succeeded in confusing and screwing myself up even more.

During this period of enforced staying in Australia because of conscription, I just wanted to escape. Travel presented itself as a means of escape. I began saving for a trip overseas. The plan was to go travelling for a year, hoping to get away from myself. I was searching for what I was too afraid to face. But I also did want to travel, to see something of the world. With the exception of war service travel, no one in my family had left Australia. My grandfather, Pop, went back to Scotland with his brother,

Louis, to visit the family in Aberdeenshire after the war, but that was likely it for the family. Travel would make me the first of my generation and the only one alive to venture beyond Australian shores.

So, I worked, which helped me save. Work and alcohol helped me get through the days and distracted me from my fears and anxiety.

At one stage I had a job at the North Sydney Leagues Club. I worked the Saturday night and Sunday morning shifts. Saturday nights I worked in the gaming bars mostly, selling beers and getting drink orders for the poker players. I'd hardly call it playing — it was an addiction. People would sit staring at the whirring wheels, never socialising, until the machines were switched off at 1:30 a.m. Next morning, I would be back for the morning shift at 10:00 a.m. as the doors were open. I saw the concentration on their faces, the same people from the night before, as they surged through the doors and headed straight for the same poker machine they were using the night before when they were switched off.

The experience cured me of ever wanting to gamble. I saw the evidence of addiction and its effect on the gamblers. I knew I was addicted to nicotine and to alcohol to an extent, but they were both legal. Though addiction to drugs and alcohol presented themselves as a possibility to me, I filed this experience away as a warning to not get too involved with other drugs.

On the Sunday shift I was employed in the auditorium. Imagine a beautiful sunny summer Sunday outside while over 1000 men, all drinking schooners, smoking and eating huge trays of prawns while they watched a sometimes bawdy and risqué show on the stage, sat inside. Why were they here? Why weren't they with their wives and children or at the beach? Instead they were crammed into a huge hall yahooing over the barely covered girls performing on the stage. That experience also cured me of schooners and platters of prawns for many years.

By this stage I was back living permanently in Sydney, flatting with various combinations of friends or lost souls, working at my boring office job in Alexandria, which was a hot, smelly industrial area a little south of the CBD. I wasn't progressing, just doing a job in order to live, drinking, smoking dope when it was available, having the occasional mediocre sex and knowing why it was mediocre.

I had been working, which gave me something to do. Besides my full-time day job, I spent various times working in pubs and sometimes clubs, filling in time and saving for my trip overseas.

During the years before I went overseas I used this time to go to dance classes at Cor and Anita De Rett's studio in Kent Street, where I did modern dance, jazz ballet and also classical. Similarly, I went to Bodenweiser Studio in City Road for modern and Indian, and to the NSW Dance Company classes at Woolloomooloo. I loved it because it was good exercise, but at the same time felt challenged by what I was doing. Why was I doing this? Why was I exposing myself to this environment? It challenged me, but I also felt comfortable in some way. I felt in some way I wanted someone to "discover" me and offer me a job, but I also felt that I did not have what it took to be a professional dancer.

Even though I was one of few men who went regularly to classes I liked being there and going through the exercises that all dance students have to do. In fact, Cor used to delight in walking around the barre while he was instructing and grabbing the students' arses and bouncing them up and down. He loved mine as he said I had floppy cheeks but really it was in good humour. I met several women my age there who I have since run into over the intervening years and we've had a good laugh at our contortions and dreams. I would have loved to be a good enough dancer to go further, but I knew even then that I didn't have the skills. Even years later into middle adulthood I have enjoyed going to the occasional dance class for adults run by the NSW Dance Company. I find it great exercise and good body discipline.

Chapter Eighteen

Getting Out

While I couldn't leave the country because of conscription, I worked extra jobs to save the money to travel. Working extra jobs as bartender and steward to save money I had enough to at least get a ticket out of the country.

I was fortunate that when Gough Whitlam was elected Prime Minister in 1972 one of his first actions was to abolish conscription. I was out of the army like a shot and never went back. That was one of the many welcome initiatives of Whitlam and his left-wing government. He was such a breath of fresh air on the political scene of Australia and implemented so many beneficial initiatives that changed the social and political fabric of Australia.

By the time Whitlam was elected I had saved enough money to leave the country. I was released from my obligation to conscription and never went back — not even to return my uniform and equipment. It was such a relief as it meant I could go overseas unhindered by any obligation to Australia.

Wanting to improve my education I finally stuck with and completed a four-year, two-nights-a-week certificate at Sydney TAFE. Achieving this proved to myself that I could achieve something that required brain power. The course was a bit of a grind, but I did it, and with good passes. I finished this in 1972. By that stage, working extra jobs as bartender and steward to save money, I had enough to travel to Europe.

I'd decided Europe was a goal some years before and told Mum that's what I wanted to do. I was surprised when she responded, "You do it then." That was a positive and encouraging response. I had decided even then that it was a way of "running away" from the life I had here.

I had made some good friends when I worked as a clerk in the state public service. We kept in touch and met up and occasionally went to a dance club, strictly in couples of course. We talked of going to London as many did, and somehow David, one of the group I got on well with, and I decided we would go to London and then on to Europe. I'd worked and saved hard until I had enough to take the plunge and get a ticket.

David and I went to Thredbo on a skiing holiday for a few days while we were saving and planning our trip overseas. I had never experienced the exhilaration of skiing. It was the first sport that I could do as well as anybody else, that I could enjoy, and one where I was not competing with anyone else. I absolutely loved it, was good enough at it and could enjoy it by myself. It was brilliant. I could ski so fast downhill, down trails in the trees, over moguls!

Once, I followed some trails that went between two big rocks. I hit the shute and flew between them, unable to stop or slow myself against the rocky walls beside me. I had no alternative but to let my body go with it. I came out the other end airborne! Much to my surprise, I landed on my back on a snow drift. Some other skiers came over to check I was okay and I just laid there staring at the blue sky, relieved I was still in one piece and able to move. That experience showed me I could be good at something physical and enjoy a sport I felt comfortable with.

Chapter Nineteen

To London!

Finally, the day came when David and I flew to London on a big Qantas plane; it was a great experience. I was so excited about the novelty of it all, my first time on a jumbo jet. I loved the meals with all the little dishes, foods and drinks that were so different to what you get served up now, especially in economy class (which is all I can afford). I loved the experience of getting settled into my little cocoon, having a cool gin and tonic, and telling myself that soon I would be on the other side of the world.

We flew into London Heathrow then navigated the Tube to the CBD. We found our way to Blackfriars, right near St. Paul's Cathedral. We had booked into the youth hostel there so we had somewhere to stay. It was near The Embankment, Blackfriars, The Strand. We could walk everywhere — to the Thames or to the tiny London pub on the corner of the lane to experience drinking pints of bitter.

I was a wide-eyed boy from the bush on Stannix Park Road! I instantly fell in love with London and immediately felt relaxed and at home, like I belonged there. David and I walked and wandered wide-eyed at the fact of actually being in London, somewhere I had dreamt about for years and that had come true. We went to the galleries, the museums, the Tate, the Tate Modern, the British Museum. We rode the Tube; the Piccadilly and Circle lines, walked the city, the shops of Oxford Street, along the Thames River. It was just like being on the Monopoly board, only real.

After a few days we bought an old Kombi at the van market and spent the next few days fitting it out with a platform for a bed, storage underneath, a camper stove, water bottles, cookware and basic supplies. We were ready to set off north to familiarise ourselves with the van and see something of Britain before we headed over the channel.

We hadn't gone far when we picked up some hitchhikers and continued north through the midlands and into the Lake District. It was the start of a holiday in another world. Here the engine carked it — totally blew up. The hitchhikers soon departed, and we were left with a week's delay in Carlysle and a hefty slug out of our travel money to get the whole motor replaced. After that it went like a dream.

We continued up into Edinburgh and explored the first old city we had seen; a beautiful, almost medieval, city. The castle and battlements, the art gallery, the narrow streets, the tiny pubs. Then up to Aberdeen, the city of my grandfather.

While in Aberdeen I located the Registrar of Births, Deaths and Marriages in the centre of town. I was interested in finding something about my grandfather's history and perhaps following this up later when I had time. The clerk found an entry for Pop's birth in 1888. The information on it gave his mother's name, and as father, the name of the man his mother had been married to. She had several of his children but had died twelve years before Pop was born. A puzzle! And a quaint way of saying Pop was a bastard. This indicated to me that his mother, my great-grandmother, had an affair with another man and had Pop as a result. Later family gossip indicated that the real father could have been her husband's brother. However, Pop was registered as having been born illegitimate and had an older brother, Louis, who he was close to and travelled back to Australia with after the end of the War about 1919. Louis probably had the same father, as he was born sometime after my grandmother's legitimate husband had died. However, their birth status appears to have affected the older family's attitude to both of them; black sheep in the family.

Years later, Aunty Peg visited the descendants of the original grandmother and grandfather, her cousins. She reported being very disappointed at their response to her, and this information would explain why; they would have looked down on Peg as being descended from a black sheep of the family. I never discussed this with Aunty Peg after I returned, and now wish I had. Another family secret.

David and I were keen to get across the English Channel to Europe so we headed for the channel ferry. As I drove off the ferry at Calais it was a real challenge to remember to drive on the righthand side of the road and to do it properly.

We were keen to get to our first European city, so we drove straight up to Amsterdam. We found the campground, full of other travellers' vans, booked in and readied ourselves to go into the city. On the way out of the driveway I kicked an envelope that was on the ground and thought it had something in it. It did. When I opened it there was a sizeable lump of hash; what a gift in the city of open marijuana use! Of course, we went back to the van and smoked some of it. Just as well not all of it at the one time! We never made it into the city that afternoon.

We did make it into the city the next day. I was blown away by how unusual Amsterdam was. The canals, houses, boats, people on bicycles everywhere. We sat on the steps of a monument in the middle of a street along with other young students. Our conversation with them was enlightening, they were speaking to us in perfect English, and each admitted to speaking several languages; here we were from Australia and we could only manage one.

After Amsterdam we headed to Denmark and into Copenhagen, a clean and friendly city, and then across the sea to Gottenberg on a huge ferry. We drove up the west coast of Sweden into Norway and Oslo, where the food was so expensive and the cost of alcohol prohibitive. We headed into the fjord country of the west coast and drove into the mountains in the middle of the country. I had never seen such mountains, the impact of centuries of glacial activity in the country. David and I exclaimed to each other as we drove along these narrow winding roads as they negotiated the steep mountains and valleys.

At one stage we drove to the end of a track that ended in a fjord at the base of a glacier with a glacial lake below. The grandeur was so impressive; in the heat and humidity of summer in Norway the lake looked so inviting. I didn't hesitate to strip to my underwear and dive into the lake. I literally dived out almost immediately, at least as fast as I could! I have never abandoned a swim as quickly as I did on that occasion. The water was freezing! No wonder of course; it came straight off the melting glacier. This was a good lesson to test the water temperature before I get in.

From Norway we drove into Sweden to Stockholm, a beautiful and somewhat majestic city on the harbour. Solid Scandinavian architecture and, though it was summer, the city was still chilly. Then we jumped on the ferry back to Denmark. We were interested and keen to go to West Berlin, an island city then inside the communist East Germany. So, we drove into West Germany and on to Hamburg.

Chapter Twenty

East and West

At this time, Germany was still divided into the west capitalist side and the Communist side, East Germany, and Berlin was the same. We caught the train from Hamburg to West Berlin. The East German police checked our passports on the train. They were quite confronting and abrupt in checking our passports and visas and grilling us on the purpose of our visit to West Berlin. They demanded to know why we were travelling through East Germany. This was our first experience of unfriendly Europeans, and a first in being dealt with like this with such suspicion and aggression. We were, after all, young and friendly Australians; a gift to the world, right? We were not used to being treated poorly and spoken to in such a manner.

East Berlin was a very different place. It was walled-off, with armed sentry posts around the perimeter. It was devastated and contained desolate spaces of land between the remaining city buildings and the wall. It was like being in an armed camp. The West Berliners carried on and lived their lives as if it wasn't there. Yet I suppose it was; I felt it was. I would think it impinged on their mental health and their lifestyle, separated and isolated as they were from the rest of West Germany and Western Europe.

On the train to West Berlin David and I were befriended by a young man from there who actually invited us to stay at his apartment. Surprised, we accepted and slept on his living room floor. I thought he may make a move on us, this being Berlin with its reputation for freer behaviour than we were accustomed to, yet he didn't; I was relieved. He was quietly generous and let us do our own thing.

We explored West Berlin, but I was drawn to explore East Berlin too as that was the seemingly more edgy locale of Berlin, the communist side. Western tourists were able to get a 24-hour visa to visit East Berlin, and so we could — let's do it! We decided to hire bikes and explore East Berlin in the time we had. Being naturally a bit provocative I wore a green tie-dyed T-shirt to see what reaction I got. At the time I had very blonde, hippie-length hair. I'd give them a taste of the decadent West. They couldn't touch me, could they?

We rode up to Checkpoint Charlie and the guards took our passports and directed us to the next check-point. We didn't like the fact they had our passports but obviously we had to go through. After keeping us waiting a long time they returned our passports and waved us through. When I emerged out of the check-point I was alone, David wasn't to be seen. I rode slowly along a desolate dusty street overlooked by armed sentries and observation towers.

Riding my bike at walking pace up the centre of this deserted street and keeping an eye out for David, I could see the sentries pointing their guns at me. I felt quite isolated and vulnerable. I was approached by a young sentry, much younger than me, a kid in fatigues with a machine gun over his shoulder and his finger on the trigger. The swagger and the gun were designed to intimidate me, which worked! The arrogance of a kid with a submachine gun over his shoulder and all the power. He offhandedly and brusquely directed me to "Halten!" He walked up, grabbed me by the front of my shirt and pulled me off the bike. I stayed very calm. What else to do? Here I was being dragged up the centre of this isolated street by a young thug with a machine gun. I dragged my bike behind me wondering "What next?" He dragged me for maybe thirty or forty metres, thumped me hard in the chest, let go of my shirt and casually turned and sauntered away. Mmm. "What now?" I thought.

By this time David had emerged as well. I got on my bike and slowly, so as not to arouse them anymore, rode in the direction of old East Berlin.

Some thirty years after the end of the war, East Berlin was decrepit. Buildings, those that were still standing, bore the pockmarks of the bombardments of the war. The streets, houses, buildings and squares were derelict and miserable. David and I rode quite a bit that day, up to the wall at several points, where we again had guns trained on us. We explored the shopping areas, which looked so depressed and run-down. Finally, we agreed we had made our point and seen enough so we returned through Checkpoint Charlie and into the freedom of the West.

After our few short days in Berlin we trained it back to Hamburg. The van was waiting for us, and we continued down the Rhine through the big industrial cities of West Germany. We hit Munich and the Octoberfest. I woke Sunday morning to find we had camped outside a church that was ringing its multiple bells especially loud because they knew we had hangovers solid enough to stop a goods train. We then travelled down through Switzerland, Salzburg in Austria and the salt mines, back to Switzerland and climbed the Matterhorn as far as we could go.

Then on to Venice in Italy. I fell in love with Venice as soon as I set foot in it. I loved the bridges and alleys, the canals and architecture, St Mark's Square, the Duomo. We spent four wonderful days losing ourselves in the narrow streets and tiny squares and finding our way out again. I've always thought the best way to explore and enjoy is to get lost and then find your way out again. That's what we used to do in the bush and the same applied here and many other new cities we immersed ourselves in; especially in the medinas of Morocco.

Chapter Twenty-One

Getting to Know You

David and I had been thrown together in a confined space, the cabin of the van, sleeping in our sleeping bags side by side for the past twelve weeks. We never spoke about our sexual needs or our views on sex. As far as I knew David was heterosexual, straight and amoral. When we were in Norway some weeks previously, we had both had sex with a couple of local girls we met. That was okay. I could still be straight. Being straight did away with all the need to hide or cover up my sexuality. I had never talked with David about my doubts, only pretended I was straight and acted in this way.

Once, we both had sex with a couple of older women who we met on the Riviera. They had made a line for us two single guys. Doubts had occurred to me when I observed how little David involved himself in this activity, but he went along with the deal. I found it stressful having to "perform." I wondered about him, being straight but seeming to not make much effort towards any girls we happened to meet. Mind you, neither did I obviously, but he didn't say anything to me either.

One night after dinner we were alone in the van. We had had a couple of bottles of wine and my guard was down. I noticed tension between us. We were standing and facing each other in the tiny space. Suddenly, David bent down and, after some initial fumbling, started to have oral sex with me. I was shocked but also enjoying it. After a while I did the same for him and we were both happy. Nothing was said and we climbed into our sleeping bags. When we awoke in the morning, again nothing was said, and we avoided interacting with each other. I was not unhappy this had happened and thought it would be good to have a retry in the near future. As we were driving later that day and not face to face it seemed a good time to bring up the activity of the night before. David was very quiet when I said, "Would you like to talk about last night?" He remained focussed on driving. "Well, I enjoyed it and I'm certainly not unhappy that it happened," I said.

David eventually said quietly, "I didn't like it." I knew that was a lie from his response the previous night. Then he said, "Let's drop the topic."

So, I did. I let it sit for the rest of the day. Later that night after we had eaten and were getting ready for bed I reached over and rubbed his back again. He didn't resist but he didn't return this either. After we laid side by side for a while, I tried to rub his back again. This time he rolled over to face me, so I wriggled down to give him oral sex again and he was happy for this to continue. After this we rolled over and went to sleep. The next night it was the same and we settled into a routine of sex before sleeping. This was lovely for me, something I had daydreamed about and wanted for a long time, but I wasn't sure he felt the same. After all it was obvious he still thought of himself as heterosexual. I still wanted to be seen as straight, but I also enjoyed the sex we had. Looking back, I regret not taking this as a step in the direction I needed to go, but I didn't.

This pleasant sex continued in an unspoken and unresolved way as we drove south along the Spanish coast, through the wonderful towns of Peniscola. We saw the beautiful Alhambra at Granada, through Valencia and Alicante and skirted the towns of Andalucia, Almara and Malaga. I was particularly struck by the fascinating lanes and streets of the villages and towns; the village houses, the different architecture of the main and domestic buildings and the churches, the importance of the Moorish influence evident throughout the changing architecture of the towns and villages.

We took a quick side visit to Gibraltar where the gates were locked and access blocked because Spain and Britain were fighting over the control of Gibraltar. But we did get to see some of the goats on the huge rock face, which seemed to be the main feature of the area.

Eventually we drove to the port and bought a ferry ticket for the van and the two of us to Morocco. The ferry was huge and soon crossed the straights of Gibraltar and landed us on the coast at Ceuta.

Chapter Twenty-Two

Exotic Moroc

Here we were in Africa! How exotic. In Morocco no less, even more exotic. It felt quite different: men in jellabas and women in veils walked along the roadside. A different vibe.

I was all for meeting the locals and wondered how we might achieve this. I proposed that we pick up a local person who might be hitchhiking and see where that got us. As we headed out of Ceuta on the main road to Marrakesh, we passed several locals on the road. Eventually we mustered up the courage to stop and offer one a lift. This man, several years older than us, in a kaftan and turban, climbed in. He seemed to understand a little English, so we were able to talk somewhat brokenly to him. He seemed friendly enough and was happy to be getting a lift. Eventually we understood that he was inviting us to spend some time with his family farther along the road. I was excited by the prospect of spending time with a local family, and David agreed to go along with my foolhardiness.

Morocco was a fairly open culture of marijuana growing and smoking dope. We understood that dope was reasonably easily available. There was also a heavy-handed response to drug use and smuggling by European Customs. Campground gossip hinted of travellers who had drugs hidden by the locals on or in their campervan. A customs search at the border had found them, much to the misfortune of the travellers concerned. It seemed that travellers would be pressured into smuggling out drugs in their van and later sell this on to other dealers. I felt that the risk was worth it and that we would be pretty unlucky to get caught up in this.

As it was starting to get dark, Ahmad finally directed us off the main road and on to a dirt track that went downhill into a steep-sided valley. It was pitch black by this time and we felt that we were at the mercy of Ahmad's goodwill. We could see way below that we seemed to be heading towards a solitary light in the narrow valley we were descending into. Eventually we drove into a high-walled courtyard where there were several people, including women in full hijab, standing around a campfire. Ahmad indicated that these were his family and of course we had to take his word for that!

He directed us on to a laneway farther on where we were to leave the van and we brought our sleeping bags back to the compound. Hence, the van was out of our supervision and we were aware it was a prime subject of tampering by the Moroccan family.

Ahmad took us to an upstairs room overlooking the courtyard and bid us sit on cushions and bolsters. It was very comfortable. Eventually a woman from his family brought us fried bread and mint tea for supper. It was very welcome and delicious. After we had eaten and felt relaxed, he passed around a hash pipe which again was devoured greedily if somewhat apprehensively.

We were both soon very stoned and comfortably immovable, ensconced on the cushions in the upstairs room. I was apprehensive, as I'm sure David was, about our safety as we were well and truly at the mercy of Ahmed and his family. The men talked to us about our willingness to smuggle drugs back to Europe, but we firmly refused. Smuggling drugs in the campervan back to Europe was certainly not our intention, yet here we were isolated and vulnerable, with people who had talked to us about taking drugs back to Europe with us. We were emphatic in refusing this but still felt that they wanted us to agree to do this for them. Here we were accepting their hospitality but not prepared to try and make life easier for them.

Our van was also vulnerable and at their mercy, unprotected and out there in the dark. We agreed they could hide anything they liked on our van and we would be none the wiser. After a delicious supper of middle eastern dishes and flavours, the family departed, and we settled down to sleep.

On awaking the next morning, the dawn light was coming in through the windows, the cocks were crowing in the courtyard. I looked out of the window to a beautiful early morning view of mist on the hillsides, chickens in the yard and a couple of family women frying what looked like doughnuts or bread on the fire. This was our breakfast, which was served soon after. Delicious fresh bread, sauces for dipping and sweet mint tea. We were both quite humbled by the hospitality we had received and discomforted by the fact that we were refusing to do what they wanted and couldn't repay their generosity in any way.

So, after grateful thanks we made our way to the van and retraced our route up to the main road. One of the men from the family hitched a lift up the hill with us. After we dropped our passenger off, we stopped beside the road and did a somewhat cursory check of the van and didn't notice anything that looked suspicious or tampered with, though truthfully we didn't know what we were looking for. So, we relied on the honesty of the family we had stayed with.

After our little cultural adventure, we were on our way to Marrakech. It is one of the major towns in Morocco, yet it was a very old city inasmuch as it had an old town, the casbah, and very little evidence of Western influence. With the help of the *Lonely Planet Guide* we found a campground where we could leave the van in relative safety and make our way through the old city and the casbah. What a wonderful eye opener the casbah was; we entered a seemingly endless maze of incredibly narrow lanes that were crowded with pedestrians. There were locals and westerners, goods of every description, vibrant colours, tiny workshops, tradesmen, weavers and tailors, and aromas suffused with a wonderful energy and vitality.

We drove on to Fez, another wonderful market city like Marrakech. The most exotic casbah was in the centre of the city and we spent lots of money on unusual and different objects to take home. Then after a wonderful experience of exotic Morocco we drove on to Ceuta and headed for Spain.

Chapter Twenty-Three

The Road to London

Our faith in the honesty of the Moroccan family was rewarded as, with relief, we didn't have any difficulty at Spanish Customs and were able to proceed.

Once back in Spain, we drove to Cordoba and Seville. Again, both beautiful Moorish-influenced cities, or really large towns. By Lisbon we had three girls hitching with us, one English and two Kiwis, so the van was pretty full. David and my sexual activity had died a natural death.

We were running short of funds so we splashed out and bought an oversupply of canned sardines because they were cheap and we could survive on them for the next few weeks. We drove up through San Sebastien and into France and Bordeaux and then to Chartres, which had a very ornate and spectacular cathedral. Then on to Paris. The girls had left us sometime along the road and we agreed to meet up again in London.

Paris was spectacular, especially the old city. Notre Dame Cathedral, the Louvre Art Gallery, l'Orangerie Gallery. Our visit was overshadowed by the fact that we had very little money and what we did have had to last us until we got back to the London banks where we could access more cash. So, we spent a few days in Paris for our first visit and decided to head for London. This took a little over a day as we drove to Calais, purchased our ferry ticket to England and drove on London.

It took a few days until we both had a room in a flat with others and we cleaned up the van and sold it at the traveller's van market near Borough Market. So, once that all had been sorted and sold David moved elsewhere. It was the end of our acquaintance. I haven't seen anything of him since then.

I moved into a flat with other Aussies at Shepherd's Bush. I loved it there. I always feel more at home in a grotty older place. It was an old house that had been wallpapered and had gone mouldy, but the people were friendly and easy going so I was happy there. It was good to be in the company of Aussies and Kiwis all sharing our overseas adventures.

With their help I registered with a local job search company and landed an office job in Olympia — a short Tube ride away — and settled into being an Aussie working in London. I was running the office within three weeks of starting there, getting some money together and thinking of travelling again. I told the boss what I was planning and said if he offered me a job with more pay that I couldn't refuse I would stay and help him out. He didn't so I left.

I loved living in London with a group of Aussies who were all enjoying their life abroad. We went to the pub, listened to music, had dinner parties. We did the tourist thing around London. Visited the art galleries and museums. I still had the usual anxiety about my sexuality, worried that others would notice me or think I was gay, that they would be judgemental of me.

At least I was earning some money and that helped fund a trip to Vancouver in Canada to visit a fellow traveller, Sara, whom I met in Europe. I went skiing at Whistler Mountain with Sara and her friends. They were great and showed me the best runs. It was such a change being confident in keeping up with competent others in a strange environment.

From Vancouver, I travelled south by bus to California and stayed in San Francisco for four days at the YMCA. This was a gay hangout, but my old paranoia had returned, and I was too nervous to indulge in any "untoward" behaviour. Much to my later regret.

I hitched to Los Angeles and met up with the family of another girl, Laura, whom we had met in Europe. We went to Disneyland for a day. It was good except I had the most awful headache all day we were there. They also took me to Hollywood and Universal Studios for the day, which was interesting and fun, but my headache was so bad I had difficulty enjoying myself. I think it was a headache brought on by depression and anxiety. I was still so anxious all the time and this played into my insecurity and anxiety.

After leaving Laura and her family I got on the freeway and hitched north out of Los Angeles. At this time there was a shooter loose on the freeways of LA randomly shooting at hitch-hikers. With my usual fatalism I decided to ignore this as my view was that if it was going to happen then it would happen, but chances are it wouldn't. I stuck my thumb out and got a lift with three interesting people who were heading north along the coast road through Sanur.

This was an interesting drive, very scenic. I knew the people I was with were perplexed that I didn't make a line for either of the two young women travelling with us. So, we got to San Francisco and I continued hitch-hiking farther north. By the time I reached Northern California I was tired of interacting with the people giving me a lift, so I caught a bus all the way north to Vancouver. I was quite relieved to be on the plane and heading back to London. The trip to North America had been an attempt to follow up on two women I had met in Europe and both attempts were pretty pointless though I had experienced some great skiing. It was my own anxiety and lack of confidence that marred what could have been an enjoyable experience.

I didn't feel this trip had been such a great success, and I was pleased to be heading back to London where I wanted to feel I belonged. I did feel much more comfortable.

Dad had kept contact with an old friend from Germany, Hanz, that he worked with at Warragamba Dam many years previously. Hanz had visited us at Stannix Park Road a few times and then he returned to Germany to live with his mother in Frederikshavn. While overseas I contacted Hanz with the intention of visiting him in Germany and having the opportunity of living with a German family.

When I collected my mail from Australia House there was an invitation from Hanz asking me to come and visit he and his mother in Frederikshavn, in Western Germany. It seemed like a good idea!

Chapter Twenty-Four

An Unassuming Brush with Fame

I caught the train from London to Frederikshavn, a long trip but enjoyable — something completely different. It was December, the depths of winter and on the way over the Channel it was extremely rough. There were passengers getting thrown across the deck, sliding down the sloping decks and ramming into benches. I tried to go downstairs to find a secure spot but the stench of vomit at the entrance drove me back. I wedged myself in between a bench and the wall of the boat with my suitcase holding me in. I stayed like that for the whole trip watching as passengers got hurled across the upper decks and slammed against the wall of the boat. After that the train to Frederikshavn was luxury.

Hanz and his mother were very welcoming, and I planned to stay with them for ten days. A few days into the stay I got really sick and had a fever. Mrs. Doll gave me a drink that tasted like sour milk and made me worse. They took me to a medical centre, and I stayed overnight. It was cold and sterile. I was alone and not understanding the language. It was a weird experience to be in a foreign hospital.

Hanz was also a skier and offered to take me skiing in Switzerland. I was surprised at this offer but accepted as I wouldn't get another chance. He and I drove down to Diavolezza, which happened to be just up the valley from the upper-class resort of St. Moritz! At the time I don't think I appreciated what this meant, or what it would have cost Hanz. Anyway, he was very generous in subsidising my skiing trip to Diavolezza.

We skied together daily on the slopes of the valley, catching the light rail train up the valley from where we were staying to the various ski slopes and cable-cars. On Saturday, Hanz announced he would not ski that day as it was his "sabbath — day of rest" so I went out myself. I caught the light rail along the valley to St. Moritz for the day and enjoyed going up in the chairlifts and skiing down again, alone with the mountains and the snow. I rekindled my love of skiing, a sport I was good at, could enjoy, and I didn't have to be compared with anyone else.

Early in the afternoon I was skiing near this couple, an older man and a younger woman who I took to be his daughter or perhaps a niece. Hearing them speaking I detected an Australian accent, albeit a cultured one! I began talking to them and they were relaxed and responded, and we spent a very pleasant afternoon skiing together.

At the end of the day we skied down to the valley, and I was a bit dismayed to realise that the last train had gone. I was looking a bit perplexed when they asked me how I was getting back to my accommodation and I told them the last train had gone. They said they were waiting for their car to arrive and would be happy to give me a lift down the valley to where I was staying. Of course, I accepted.

The car soon arrived, and I was quietly impressed that it was a huge, wide Mercedes sedan, a bigger car than any I had been in. He offered to put my skis on the roof racks, and I got in the front with the driver and him. An adult woman, whom I assumed was his wife, the young woman we had been skiing with and a young boy around early teenage years were in the back. When we got to where I was staying, he hopped out and removed my skis. I thanked him very much for the afternoon and the lift home, and then asked him his name. "Rupert Murdoch," he said. I was a bit stunned to say the least and I knew I should know the name but for the moment didn't connect. I lamely replied "Oh. Nice to meet you," or words to that effect, and they drove off.

Later I realised I had been skiing with Rupert Murdoch, the media mogul and his daughter Elizabeth. This was really at the start of his power and influence, which later turned sour. His wife, Anna, was in the back seat with his son, Lindsay. It was amazing that they seemed so relaxed, friendly and easy. I realised, too late to say anything, that he had been very supportive of Whitlam at election time and used his considerable media power and influence to support his campaign. Whitlam's election had made my life so much easier.

Of course, when he turned that power and influence to oppose Whitlam's re-election after the dismissal and subsequent Murdoch media gutter press, my feelings towards him and his empire turned to disappointment and frustration.

However, a notable brush with fame.

Chapter Twenty-Five

A Grecian Idyll

Once I was back in London for a few weeks, it was getting close to the time I needed to be thinking of heading home again. I was running short of cash to keep living in London and experiencing the usual anxiety I felt when cash was getting low. I didn't feel I had achieved as much as I would have liked while overseas. My sexual identity issues, anxiety and depression had not improved, and my confidence was very low. Not a promising way to return to Australia. I also knew I would return to the same boring dead-end job I had left those many months before.

For someone running out of money and experiencing anxiety issues London was so expensive! I did try going back to work, but this wasn't appealing. I was feeling very flat and unmotivated at the thought of my overseas holiday drawing to a rapid close, not having much money left, not knowing how much I needed to see me through and not having made any headway on dealing with my identity issues. I wanted to do something to get me out of myself on the way home. But what to do?

I decided to head to Greece for a short holiday before flying home as I hadn't been there. The cheapest and most direct was by bus to Athens so I spent some of the remainder of my cash on a bus ticket to Athens. This gave me just enough for a week somewhere cheap in Greece and the cost of my flight ticket home. However, I was not in a good space to be making these decisions.

When I arrived in Athens, I still had to swap all my remaining travel cheques for cash so I could buy the return ticket to Sydney. It was all the money I had left, and I was not emotionally ready to go home yet.

Feeling very low I went to a bank in Athens near the travel agent to cash my remaining cheques. I began signing the cheques in front of a teller and immediately had what seemed to be a panic attack. I froze, I couldn't stop shaking, every signature was in a different scrawl and I couldn't sign the remaining cheques. I was freaking out that the teller would not give me my money, that I wouldn't be able to pay for my ticket. Luckily, he could see I was in a state and let me sit down for a while. After I had settled myself down, he allowed me to come back and finish signing the cheques and gave me the money. I was so relieved when that was done. I went straight to the travel agent nearby and paid for my ticket to Sydney. Qantas flew directly from Athens to Sydney in those days, so I knew I was on the way and it had been paid for.

I had left myself about a week before I flew out. I still had a few dollars left and I wanted to get out of Athens and go to a Greek island for the reminder of my time to rest and relax. Feeling very anxious and unhappy I went down to the port, Piraeus, and paid for the cheapest ticket that would get me to an island. Hydra was only a few hours by ferry from Piraeus so that was it. As the ferry sailed into the port of Hydra, I knew that was a good choice. Hydra had a beautiful, quiet harbour lined with low-key buildings, a few boats, evidence of a few local tavernas on the waterfront, the village rising from the harbour up a steep hillside. As we disembarked there were locals hawking accommodation and donkeys waiting to take luggage. There were no taxis or motorised transport on the island; everything was by foot or donkeys.

I approached a local woman who had a room to let with a cheap tariff, which I accepted. I didn't know at the time it was a share room with another young man about eighteen years old from California; an early starter on the travel scene. This was fine with me and he proved to be an amiable roommate. Of course, nothing happened. I met another young gay couple and ached to talk to them about my dilemma but was not able to, much to my regret.

I spent the days wandering around the village, sitting in a local taverna, reading, doing some sketching. I was filling in time and feeling morose at the end of my trip. On the last morning of my visit I was sitting in the taverna when the gay couple joined me. They told me they had been wondering about me and asked in a most caring way if I was gay. They said they were happy to talk if I wanted to. I was running out of time until the ferry left for Piraeus and blurted out that I would love to talk and burst into tears. Too late, though, to allow them into my "secret," as I was leaving that morning.

Chapter Twenty-Six

Home Again, Home Again. Jiggety-Jig

My travels in Europe were over, and I boarded the plane at Athens Airport. As I entered the cabin, the Aussie steward said, "Welcome aboard." His accent was so broad and welcoming I was really chuffed and said to him, "How good to hear your accent!"

So, what was I returning to? I hadn't found the guts to do anything proactive about my sexuality. I still felt scared of myself, of what I was trying to deal with. So, when I arrived back in Australia, I was depressed, miserable and unhappy at being back. The most depressing part was not having another job to go to other than the boringly tedious job in the personnel department at Stores and Transport in Alexandria. Was I just returning to my same old life as before, no changes, still living in fear of myself and everybody else?

However, it was an exciting time politically in Australia, with the progressive left-wing Whitlam government having implemented lots of overdue and welcome reforms. I felt a new energy for the political future of Australia. There was lots of money for the arts and other areas that had been neglected and held back by years of stale conservatism.

Viv, someone I had known since primary school days at Glossodia, had been working at the Stores and Transport branch at Alexandria. She told me about a job happening at the Australia Council for the Arts. I had never heard of this part of the public service before, but then found out a colleague from my previous job at Stores and Transport would be my boss if I got a job there. Whitlam poured lots of money into the promotion of all forms of art and artistic endeavour. I had enjoyed doing the dance classes and training in the late 60's and early 70's, so I applied for a job in the Dance Board. The person appointed had a degree in dance, so I never got a look in there, but my interest was spiked.

At my interview the Chief Administration Officer, an ex-army type I found out much to my dismay, asked me what book I was reading. Fortunately, at the time I happened to be reading *Cancer Ward* by Alexander Solzynetskin, which sounded impressive although I don't recall if I ever finished it. However, I was pleased to note he seemed appropriately impressed (I wonder if he really knew the book as he seemed to at the time?) and I landed the job of Assistant Administration Clerk in the Administration Section, second to my ex-boss at Stores and Transport Alexandria. My job was to organise travel and accommodation for project and board staff while they were away visiting arts bodies interstate, assist in a minor way with organising and catering for visiting dignitaries, and process payment of accounts and reimbursements and so on. It was a lot of work but the world into which I moved was a great distance from where I had come from at Stores and Transport Alexandria.

Chapter Twenty-Seven

Life at the OzCo

Life at the Australia Council for the Arts, or the OzCo as it was affectionately called, was frenetic and stressful and ultimately the best thing for me. It was full of extraordinary, colourful and intelligent characters, so unlike any public service types I had encountered before. At times we worked exceedingly long hours, but we also partied and had a great time.

Included in my job was organising travel and accommodation, approving expenses and payments, and compiling itineraries for the board members and staff. Working with the various boards and board staff on a daily basis introduced me to people the like of whom I had never encountered before. They all had degrees or post graduate qualifications, they were intelligent, diverse and interesting, from families in the eastern suburbs, the North Shore or Inner West. They were interested in the arts, politics and philosophy, and came from educated, often professional, affluent middle-class backgrounds, or like me, from a working-class background who had worked and studied hard to move into such an interesting area.

And of course, there was a higher percentage of gay and lesbian people who were generally very accepting of me, as everyone was. Although I was directly challenged at one stage about my sexuality. I did not feel threatened or demeaned by this. I was relaxed in my interactions with them and they with me.

The only major unpleasant experience I had at the OzCo was a time I was summoned to the administration manager's office. A well-known Sydney identity who was employed in a consultant capacity harangued me about my role in a travel payment and organisation matter that was outside my scope of responsibility. I felt insulted, hurt and angered at his arrogance in dressing me down in a bullying and demeaning fashion. The administration manager simply looked on and allowed his diatribe to run its course. I was shaken by this episode as it was unlike my interactions with staff at the OzCo both before and subsequently. Again, my response to trauma was to stand quietly and let it happen. I felt powerless, outranked and unsupported by my manager.

However, it was so exciting and mind-expanding for me, a boy from the bush with such a limited life experience. The experience I did have before this was limited by fear, insecurity and a sense of unworthiness. I realised that these people were treating me as an intelligent human, their intellectual and social equal. They were interested in my opinions, they invited me to join them for lunch and to functions in their homes. I was amazed and I loved it. No one had ever done this for me before. I realised that I, too, could do this, and it was up to me to make my part in it. They also voiced political and social justice views that aligned with mine and encouraged my feelings of equality and acceptance. This made me more decisive and confident in accepting and voicing my own left-leaning views on politics and social change. These feelings of acceptance and equality were so different to what I had experienced before. I felt appreciated.

However, it was also evident that I needed an education. I felt confident from my interactions with colleagues at the OzCo and with the completion of my TAFE course. I must have had a reasonable intellect otherwise they would not bother with me, so I began seeking higher education.

After doing a non-graduate year in anthropology at Sydney Uni I realised I could handle a university level of academic work. I decided to leave work and enrol in a four-year full-time teaching degree at Macquarie University.

After I landed the job at the OzCo I wanted to live in the city independently so I rented a flat at Lavender Bay that looked out over the waters of Sydney Harbour. What a glorious spot. But I was lonely and unhappy with myself when I was not distracted and busy working. Eventually I moved into another flat at North Sydney with two women from work. That was better but they were not partners for me.

After work, if I wasn't doing anything, I got into the habit of going up to Kings Cross and I would go to a nightclub called the Pink Pussycat and listen to music and dance on the podium. Early in the evening there was no-one there and I had the place to myself. I felt weird but elated at dancing like a dervish to the Bee Gees and LaBelle but I loved it. I secretly hoped someone would discover me but nothing ever happened. It was fun and I enjoyed it but it was totally avoidance behaviour.

Soon after my return from Europe I met a young woman my age named Maureen. She was a friend of the people I had shared a house with at Shepherd's Bush in London. I was still very lonely and searching, so I easily fell into a relationship and engagement. She lived in county Victoria and we saw each other intermittently, having a long-distance affair. Meanwhile, I continued to live my life in Sydney. She visited a few times to the house I was sharing, which was a short drive from Macquarie, but we had little personal contact. It was more of a long-distance phone relationship.

I soon knew I had made a disastrous decision to become engaged to someone I didn't really know and with whom I had little in common. I agonised how to resolve it. I knew that to continue would be worse than disastrous for us both and very unfair on the unsuspecting Maureen. As the weeks passed, I twisted myself into a tangle of anxiety.

I was still searching for my own identity, of course. I wanted a wife, kids, a house, a career, a life to share with someone I loved and who loved me; someone to go through life with. I knew this was incompatible with a gay life, but I thought it would be an answer to my loneliness and longing. That's what everybody wanted and what so many of my friends sought and were successful at. Why couldn't I? I knew I could do it; I knew I wanted to do it and I found I could follow that path and forget about the other issues that were at the back of my mind. I pushed them there and didn't want them to affect my desire for a hetero-normal relationship, partnership, children and career.

I know now why I chose a teaching career and not an arts-based career. This would have meant I could have moved back into the arts areas of the Australia Council. My fears of discovery and that I would face challenges to my sexuality that I would find too confronting swayed my choices. I took the less threatening route in that respect. But Maureen was not the answer.

Chapter Twenty-Eight

Finding a Soulmate

I met Maeve at the Australia Council. She had just been appointed as Secretary to the Crafts Board. She was immediately friendly, interesting and interested in me. Others were interested too, but somehow Maeve was different. She was talented and bright, intelligent and hard-working, and she held great left wing political and social justice views. Maeve had held a top trade union position in the Actors Union in London, England, where she had lived for seven years. She had travelled and lived overseas. She was from a country background, from a middle-class grazier family, yet she was down to earth, warm and interesting to be with. Most of all, she seemed interested in talking to me.

Maeve began to tick all the boxes. I got to know her at a work level and went to her house for after work parties and dinners with lots of our colleagues. I really enjoyed being with these people, they were interesting, vibrant, good politically, passionate about the arts and arts practice, and they had a great time relaxing after work. And Maeve was there amongst them. However, I still had the unresolved issue of my relationship with Maureen.

Friends at the Australia Council would often go out partying after work and I often accompanied them.

They were such a good bunch of interesting and vibrant people. This occasionally continued even after I had left the OzCo and was by then a student at Macquarie Uni. I was living in a share house at Drummoyne, a short drive from Macquarie Uni. One Friday we ended up at Maeve's house in Paddington for drinks and possible dinner. I had been there before and was excited at the prospect of socialising with friends from my old work.

Late that night Maeve made a move on me, but I begged off with a headache and went home, thinking "What a wimp!" I wondered what she must think of me. What a wuss! But I did have a pounding headache at the time, maybe exacerbated by the pressure of being asked to stay and what that meant for my reputation as a man. I also knew that I had some unfinished business to be sorted out before I embarked on another sexual and romantic encounter!

After the night of the party at Maeve's I was in a state of indecision for several weeks. Eventually, I summoned the courage to make a phone call to Maeve and, after I'd said who was calling, realised she didn't even know who was speaking to her. After it dawned on her who it was, I said nervously, "I owe you a dinner." Eventually, the penny dropped and she responded, "No you don't." It was not easy dealing with these independent feminist women!

"Yes, I do," I replied. "I want to repay you for that one at your place some weeks ago"

"Oh," she said. "Okay. Where?"

Trying to sound like I had some sophistication I nominated a French restaurant off Oxford Street. She agreed and we made a date. I was exhausted and elated. These feminists were not easy to convince!

That Friday we went to Le Poulet and had a really relaxed and pleasant date. Maeve was easy to be with, vivacious, intelligent. We talked and laughed about work, the arts, politics in Australia, about London, life and travel, the similarities of our background growing up in the country and our differences. I was impressed with her non-judgemental ability to accept without comparison and enjoy my company.

As the evening progressed, I noticed that Maeve had begun weeping quietly.

"What's the matter?" I asked, concerned.

"I'm just thinking that here is another lovely young man and he will probably go the way of the rest of them," she sobbed.

I was hooked. I knew I could not let this woman down — that I didn't want to — and that she was all the things I had been asking the universe for. On the way back to her place she was still weeping in the car so I stopped and asked if she would be more comfortable if I put the seat back, which I did (duh!). Instead the seat went all the way back and she nearly choked as I struggled to right the seat. This was good for a laugh and she relaxed and settled down. We drove back to her place, and after she did some convincing at the front door, I stayed and that was it.

The next day after a late start I drove south. I had decided to drive to Victoria and break off the engagement to Maureen. I drove all day and arrived late afternoon. I had rung to say I was coming and that I wanted to discuss something with her. I also rang the friend from London that we had in common and asked her to join us as a support for Maureen. We met in town. I saw her and told her what I had decided and why and that it was for the best that we not continue with the engagement. She was understandably devastated and angry.

After I could leave, I was so relieved I drove all the way back to Sydney without a break. I went to Maeve's place and stayed the remainder of the weekend. I felt remorse for what I had done to Maureen, but such relief at the decision I had made and acted on. I felt I'd done the right thing at last and my actions had brought me back to Maeve. The future again looked bright and positive. Maeve was an intelligent and compassionate woman, politically sound, with the same social justice viewpoint I had. All the attributes I admired. She wanted a relationship that included sharing our life, children and equality.

Chapter Twenty-Nine

Being a "Mature Age" Student

By the time Maeve and I got together I was already at Uni. I was twenty-nine and Maeve was thirty-three. While still at the OzCo I had done the year of a non-degree course in anthropology at Sydney Uni and that had been successful. I felt it showed to me at least that I could handle that level of brain work!

At the end of that non-degree year I decided that if I was going to go to university I wanted to go full-time, experience the life of a student, and immerse myself in it — as far as my inhibitions would let me, that is.

Also, being a working-class boy from a fairly non-educated background, I wanted to do a degree that I knew I could use, that was practical and appropriate, and one in which I could develop a career. So, I chose a four-year teaching degree at Macquarie University. I combined that with psychology as it was a popular choice at the time (and still is), so in the end I had a double major. I also concentrated on primary teaching as I didn't think I wanted to deal with "those uppity teenagers" in high school. That wish came back to haunt me!

Maybe I should have proceeded into an arts degree but at the time a teaching degree seemed much more practical and fitted my needs for security and a steady income.

In those days there were a number of people who could consider university study because it was free, and the government offered a student allowance. There were conditions, however. I was conditionally enrolled as a non-matriculated student, which meant I had to pass all of Year 1 to obtain a matriculation and full enrolment status. I wandered around campus in a sort of unknowing daze in the first semester, thinking that here I was almost thirty, surrounded by so many younger people. I didn't know anyone, I had no job, no career, no relationship (as yet) and I didn't even know how to write an essay! I quickly fixed the latter problem and wrote my first essays after attending a student workshop. I felt a great sense of achievement when I passed the first year with admirable results.

In addition to the teaching and psychology courses, I tacked on a few arts subjects that looked interesting. I was amazed at the freedom I had to choose from a large number of interesting courses that all counted toward what I needed — the points! I had a ball, actually. My mind expanded exponentially as I analysed poetry, taking a deep dive into the imagery and turns of phrase; the music of the form. I enjoyed the fantasy and adventure of children's literature, discussing the ancient philosophers of Greece, Rome and modern times. I actually understood a basic maths course for teaching and received distinctions in several classes.

I was amazed and thrilled. I was intellectually stimulated. I had a brain! I became the first person in my family to finish high school, travel overseas and graduate from university. Many of my younger relatives have graduated since then and left me for dead, several with master's degrees including both my sons and even one with a Medical Doctorate, but I was the first of my generation.

During that four years, I moved from being single and a non-matriculant student to my relationship with Maeve, living in our unrenovated house, married, father of our first child, and working to support us. By the time I finished the degree I was tired of studying. In retrospect perhaps I should have continued to do further study, as it would have been beneficial professionally, but at the time I wasn't keen to continue. I was eager to get a paying job and my own income. Anyway, the demands and busyness of life intervened.

It was at Macquarie Uni that I also started doing a pottery course in the Student Union. I was familiar with and liked pottery and met a few well-known potters through Maeve and the Crafts Board of the OzCo, so thought I would give it a try. I don't remember making anything remarkable in those early days, but it certainly sparked an interest and I continued to hand-build at home and fire my work either at university or later at schools I worked in. It was the start of many years of creativity and pleasure, both of which were important to me.

Chapter Thirty

Adventures in Life with Maeve

I was really happy, and I was happy to be with a woman like Maeve.

She possessed all the attributes I thought would be desirable in a partner. We shared so many similar views on politics, social justice, environmental causes and what are called "left wing" issues (I prefer to see them as a concern for other people and for the environment, as opposed to simple concern for oneself). I had found an intelligent, independent-thinking feminist who wanted a career, a family and a home.

These qualities were very important to me because I wanted to share my life with Maeve as an equal partner, and Maeve wanted this too. I was very happy to do this. I didn't want to be the "sole bread winner" or the Head of the House in the traditional sense. I wanted a relationship where we were both equal, in it together, sharing the load, the responsibilities of finance and children; independent but responsible, our own careers, and incomes and able to share all this with a partner. In the early days we did. We had it and the future looked promising!

Because I was full-time at uni I had a student allowance of about $42 a week, but I also had the energy and time to work at hospitality jobs to earn some money and pay my way. I once worked at the Hero of Waterloo at the Rocks. What a great little pub. It dated from convict days, the very early 1800's in Sydney, and had a tiny main bar. Sometimes a couple of jazz musicians would perform. I worked the frantic, noisy Friday and Saturday night shifts. I loved the energy of the workers letting loose on the weekend; it was like getting paid to attend a noisy, drunken, fun party. Sometimes we would be falling over each other trying to serve schooners to the eager revellers, all baying to be served. One time the noise and demands of the crowd were so chaotic, I yelled at the top of my voice "Shut up for a minute so we can hear your orders!" Amazingly they did, and suddenly it was quiet. They momentarily looked at me in astonishment; they weren't used to being spoken to like that by a barman. Then the chaos took over again. That job ended when a new owner took over the lease and sacked all the existing staff in one go. We never knew why.

As the end of first year of uni drew to a close, I had decided I wanted to travel to Indonesia and Thailand. I had a bit of money saved and we were single and free — no children yet! I was happy to go by myself but asked Maeve if she would like to come, and she agreed. She told me later that she had never "roughed it" as much as we did that time but also that she enjoyed it immensely. At the end of semester, we headed off to Bali to start our trip. The idea was that we would travel through Indonesia, Bali, Java and Sumatra. At Medan in northern Sumatra, Maeve would fly back to Sydney and I would continue through Malaysia and on to Thailand.

Maeve had spent many years in Britain and travelled in Europe. I had travelled in London, around Europe, and some of North America, so we were used to the vagaries of travel in unfamiliar lands. I felt fantastic travelling with a fun, interesting partner who was willing to give anything a go. We had some memorable adventures.

We rode a motorbike on the crowded roads of Bali, Maeve riding pillion. We ate on the street, slept in scrappy little losmans, climbed a volcano at dawn, saw a Royal Monkey Dance and attended a traditional wedding. We stayed in Ubud hanging out with the other travellers — the cool young things — eating banana pancakes and drinking Bintang. We got to see and do things that are too expensive to do these days.

In Yogyakarta we were invited to a traditional puppet performance. The local nobility and dignitaries sat in front of the puppets, seeing the actual figures. As westerners, we sat behind the screens and watched in fascination as the shadow puppets enacted the drama of the Ramayana. It went on for hours, but it was so enjoyable. A real privilege.

We'd heard of magic mushrooms and decided to try them. Being moderate in all things and not wanting to overdo it we ordered one mushroom omelette to share. It was a beautiful afternoon, so afterwards we went and sat on a hillside in the sun. We were both pretty stoned and I thought we were enjoying ourselves until Maeve began to groan and couldn't move from where she was lying on the grass. She was really out of it and though I was quite stoned, I was still aware and very concerned for her. The drug-induced paranoia kicked in. What if she died? What would I tell her parents, especially her father? How would I get her down from the hill? How could I get her assistance? Much to my relief she eventually woke up. We were starving by this point so we went and found a café to soothe our munchies.

There was one incident in Bali when Maeve seemed to get really tired and unwell and lay on the bed for a few days; she seemed unable to get up or have any energy. It seemed strange at the time but this being the tropics I was just concerned that she recover. She did and we thought nothing more of it. I wonder if this had any relevance to the events of later years.

Djakarta was a huge, sprawling, polluted, crowded city even then. There were great divides between the poor villagers and the massive high rises next door. It was the first Asian city either of us had encountered. We stayed with a contact of Maeve's, a woman who worked at the Australian Embassy. I'd never met a single woman who had a huge house, servants to wait on her hand and foot, and nothing to do but work, drink gin and party. We experienced what life as an expat must be like. Drunk on gin 24/7 it seemed. For three days we managed to live in an alcoholic haze, socialising and sightseeing, but then we both had to pull the plug and left Djakarta to dry out.

We flew to Padang in Sumatra on a local airline called Merpati. On the plane we sat in deck chairs that were literally screwed to the floor, while looking out at the glorious coastlines of the islands and the caldera of Krakatoa.

In Padang we weren't allowed to sleep in the same room as we weren't married, our first experience of ways of living so different from what we had worked for. Then a bus ride on narrow mountain roads through tropical rainforest to Lake Toba, a primitive and superstitious culture, then on to Medan, a huge polluted city.

Here we met up with the sister of a good friend I had known well for a number of years. She was travelling with her boyfriend and had her passport stolen. She had to remain in a Medan hotel room for several months by herself waiting for her new passport. What a lonely and frustrating thing for her to endure, but it was not an uncommon occurrence then.

After arriving in Medan, Maeve left the next day for Sydney and the day after I flew to Georgetown in Malaysia and straight into another culture shock.

I'd discovered that some good friends of mine from the share-house days in Sydney were travelling overland back from London and would be in Georgetown at the same time. It's always exciting to meet up with friends to share experiences outside of Australia and this was no exception. I teamed up with Rob and Val and we went out to the northern coast of Georgetown and stayed in a losman on the beach. This was great and just up our hippy alley. However, the Malaysian Immigrasi had a different idea for us hippies. They raided the unlicensed losmans and took our passports because we were not staying in licenced hotels. We were told that we could collect them the next day at the immigration office in Georgetown.

We rolled up to the counter in the immigration office the next day and I was handed back my passport by the clerk who seemed to really resent the fact that he had to deal with the likes of me. He abruptly informed me I was not welcome in Malaysia and had twenty-four hours to leave the country! I felt very indignant at this treatment and the manner in which it was delivered, and my response was a retort to the clerk, in a loud and annoyed voice, that I had no wish to return to their country in any case. Well! These rows of young clerks toiling away at their desks raised their faces as one and glared at me. I thought I might have overdone it a bit and meekly left. Luckily, I was at the north of Malaysia and could catch a train into Thailand very quickly. Rob and Val had a rushed twenty-four hours to travel across the length of Malaysia to get to Singapore. Thus ended a short visit to Malaysia, at that time a very conservative country both culturally and politically, and one that I was quite uncomfortable with.

After escaping Malaysia, I travelled north to Bangkok and enjoyed being alone in a huge Asian city. Travelling north to Chang Mai I joined a tour to the northern villages. We were told one of the villages we stopped in was a morphine village where there were obvious drug houses. I wanted to try it, so I went with a man into a hut and inhaled a good fill of morphine. Nothing much happened, I didn't get very stoned, but it was an edgy experience.

On the drive back, I was abused by the drunken Thai driver. I told him to slow down because he was speeding and seemed drunk or stoned or both. Now that was freaky. Again, I withdrew into the typical response of trauma and being confronted by aggression by going into shock and withdrawing into myself.

On my return from Asia at the beginning of 1977, Maeve and I found an old flat at Greenwich and started to live our life together. From Greenwich I could drive out to Macquarie Uni and Maeve had a short train ride to North Sydney. It was a beautiful spot in a once beautiful old house; sunny days, glorious trees and the shimmering water of the harbour. We were both enjoying the first days of our life together.

I was starting my second year at university and working as a barman back at North Sydney Leagues. Maeve was developing her promising career in arts administration with the Australia Council.

Chapter Thirty-One

No Time to Think

I had a block of land near my parents at Wilberforce, about eighty kilometres from Sydney, that I was paying off with the idea of eventually using that as a deposit on a house; I never entertained the thought that I would live in Wilberforce. Maeve and I discussed getting a loan and buying a house we could afford rather than paying rent. Maeve was earning a good salary, so we decided to apply to the bank for a loan. Our application depended solely on Maeve's salary because I was a lowly barman and a student. This did not deter the bank manager who interviewed us. He did not look at Maeve or address her once during the interview. His attention was solely on me as the male in the relationship. A great example of the heterosexual male-dominated society we lived in. That Maeve was a feminist was understandable; I was too, at least I called myself one. I guess I still am though political correctness has changed a lot in the intervening years.

We got the loan and bought a run-down shell of a house in Darlington. We called it Chippendale because Darlington was seen as an even worse slum than Chippendale and was just across the road! The whole area was completely run down and derelict. No trees or vegetation to speak of, rough and uneven asphalt roads and lanes, lined with rusting galvanised iron fences and falling down timber structures — completely rundown housing. Somehow, we saw the potential in the area; we could afford it and live in it while we renovated. Also, we were close to the city.

We weren't alone in having these criteria. As we moved into the area we found many young couples, straight or same sex, living in derelict houses while renovating them to a more liveable standard. The street developed a real sense of community and support; it was common for others to drop in, or for us to do the same, calling in for a cuppa or a meal, comparing tips on renovating, helping out when extra hands were needed to raise beams or demolish a room. By the time we sold up and left the area fifteen years later, the whole community had been transformed. There were trees and plants lining the street and tiny front spaces. Homes had been painted and renovated and the back lanes were cleaned up to show the now verdant back yards.

This was 1977 when housing was cheap but bank interest was high — about 18%. Somehow, we could afford it. People like us who had lots of energy and enthusiasm but not much money could buy in and renovate an old rundown house and live close to the city. We loved it; it was fun apart from everything else. We were pioneers in the rejuvenation of the inner suburbs. I really felt like I was building the future I wanted with a partner I wanted to share it with.

I knew deep down that I was avoiding the spectre of what it was I needed but didn't want. However, this was a good time for me, a time of being so busy with life that I had no time to reflect nor did I make any time to reflect on what else it was in my life that needed attention.

Our house was a two-story structure that had been built as the main house with two rooms downstairs and two rooms above. At five metres wide, it seemed quite roomy. There was a side passage of over a metre wide from the street that added to the width of the backyard, which included a couple of young trees as a bonus. The old brick dunny, thankfully unused for a number of years, sat at the back. In a separate building behind the two front rooms was a small kitchen with a lean-to bathroom at the back and one room above the kitchen accessible by a narrow staircase along the back wall of the kitchen. The bathroom was almost unusable but had water to the sink and the shower that seemed to drain OK, so we could use that. The kitchen had the old fireplace still intact and a functioning sink in the corner. There was a lean-to roof over the gap between the main section and the kitchen with a step and uneven concrete as a floor. The floorboards were so old they had buckled and been painted yellow. The walls were all brick, the old cinder bricks painted over. We found these so appealing when the paint was removed which was an arduous process of dusty chipping, chipping, chipping for hours, but worth it in the end to reveal walls of beautiful sandstock brick.

The ceilings were of the old style "wattle and daub," a mixture of plaster pushed between split sticks of "wattle" smoothed to a degree and painted with lime. The stairs led to the two bedrooms upstairs. The front room upstairs was a beautifully proportioned room with one large twelve-paned window and a set of French doors onto the balcony. It still had its iron lace though this was damaged in parts. The windows on both levels were very appealing; a large, old style with six small panes top and bottom. A gigantic, gnarled wisteria, which was not in flower when we first saw the house, grew over the balustrade. Little did we realise what a magnificent spectacle it would create when it flowered in spring.

Though it was very dilapidated and in basically original condition, we found it habitable for our needs and moved in immediately. We established that it would have been built around 1840 or even earlier. It was a free-standing house whereas houses on either side were attached terraces, so it would have been built just before they started to join the houses into terraces; it was quite roomy compared to adjoining houses. We were so proud of our first home! We adored living in the inner city of the best city in the world.

The first thing I did was rip out the stairs in the kitchen to make more space. I built a set of stairs, more a step ladder, to fit in a much smaller space and provide ready access to the room above. This was my first Do-It-Yourself project and it looked great and worked a treat. It was the first of many home renovation projects I mastered. This upstairs room became my study where I would write my essays and attempt to master the typewriter Maeve had bought for me. Meanwhile she was getting dinner in the kitchen below. Every now and then I would yell that it was "All too hard" when I hit a blind spot! I was still pretty green and inexperienced at writing an essay, arguing my point and mastering a typewriter. Ever since then I have regretted not learning to touch type!

We stumbled into our first major expense when we found that the roof was rusted through. We had a huge Sydney downpour and the water leaked all down the walls and the floors, inundating the house. Pulling off the layers of rusted iron we discovered the original timber shingles and over a century of inner-city coal dust over the lathe and plaster of the ceilings. However, the work and expense of a new roof was worth it; it sheltered us and the house itself from any further major weather events, leaving us protected to continue our lives and the renovations underneath.

The months and years flew by. I was at uni and working, doing renovations and new projects. Maeve was working at a more than full-time job, travelling interstate at times and sometimes attending late night meetings. Occasionally, I was included in socialising with board members and staff when they were in Sydney. Maeve and I had a good and busy life.

It was at these Craft Board functions that I got to know Peter Rushforth, an eminent retired potter of Sydney Art School. I later had the pleasure and honour of working with him at his studio in the Blue Mountains.

Maeve's parents lived in Albury, southern New South Wales, as they had retired from the family property in Henty in the Riverina area of NSW. They were a wealthy grazing family, though I think most of the wealth was tied up in property. The property had been left to two of the sons as chief inheritors as they had stayed on the farm, married and had families. The other siblings, two boys and three girls, left to make a life elsewhere. The boys wanted to escape the life of a rural male and the three girls because they were excluded from the inheritance because of their gender.

This did not sit well with Maeve, her younger sister Eve and her older brother Michael, who was a gay man. Michael had found it extremely hard to be an out gay man, especially to his father and some of his siblings. His dad, a Henry Parkes (icon of an Australian politician of the late 1800's) type with a long, bushy beard. He was tall, patriarchal, dogmatic, stern, authoritarian and homophobic. Michael had left for the city several years before Maeve, and he and Maeve had a really close relationship. She was supportive of him, her eldest brother, and he of her as she made her way in the city, far away from the farm. Michael introduced Maeve to the clubs, pubs, nightlife and parties of Kings Cross and Potts Point. It's a great sadness that he never came out to his parents. Maeve and I discussed this later and they must have known, especially his mother, Edith. Despite a life on the farm with an autocratic husband, she had spent her life as a loyal but independent and liberal-thinking country woman, raising seven children and feeding the family and the farm workers. She had been a music teacher and remained a talented pianist. Edith would have been able to openly accept Michael's lifestyle.

Michael sometimes used to flirt a little with me but nothing serious; he respected my role as his sister's partner and husband. I may have been tempted in the earlier months of our relationship if he had tried anything, but he never did.

Through Michael, we were invited to the occasional party around the Eastern Suburbs with friends where I felt the old stirrings arising.

By this time Maeve was rarely able to attend but would stay at home, leaving me to go by myself. That was uncomfortable for me as I remained loyal to Maeve and the family but still experienced the urges and temptations of another lifestyle.

Michael was a heavy drinker and smoker and became a total alcoholic in his later years, unable or without the will to look after himself. He spent his last years with spells in rehab and in a boarding house in Liverpool Street in Inner Sydney where he was found dead after many months of concern for him.

Edith used to come to Sydney occasionally to visit Maeve and Eve and their families. Edith was pleased to see Maeve and me in our own house and establishing a life, not paying rent. She was not so pleased to see the pretty basic conditions in which we lived; it would have seemed very primitive and sub-standard. Edith grew up in outback Victoria in the early part of the twentieth century but even so this was not how she want her daughter to be living.

We didn't have much money and we spent what we had on dining out, short trips, occasional theatre and so on. We used to buy the occasional artwork if we found one we liked and could afford. At one exhibition we bought an Ann Thompson drawing for $1100, which was a lot at the time.

When Edith saw it and heard how much we paid she was aghast. She suggested we would have been better buying carpet to cover the floorboards. Maeve replied that floor covering was not a priority and we would rather spend the money on art. "That's what I like to hear!" I thought.

Chapter Thirty-Two

Becoming Parents

We had talked about Maeve having a child. She was three years older than me, so she was feeling the pressure to act soon. I was happy to support her in this choice, so we talked about her stopping the pill. She had taken it non-stop from her mid teenage years so there was some concern that she would possibly have some difficulty getting pregnant. So, she stopped. Not long after that she announced she was pregnant! We were both overjoyed and excited; a big step in our lives together. I seemed to be moving in the direction I wanted — to lead a straight life with marriage and a family. I felt good about this but still had the ever-present feelings lurking in the background and, at this time, not acted on but repressed. Could I continue like this for the next forty years?

Maeve intended to work until a few weeks before the birth as any good feminist would. She had a pretty flawless pregnancy; a little morning sickness at the beginning, then she sailed through. She stopped smoking immediately after we decided to get pregnant and as the pregnancy proceeded, she was in glowing good health.

I was in the third year of my uni course and working practicals in schools. I sensed how teachers treated those children whose parents were not married or who had a different surname to their mother's. I did not want that sort of bias for my own children, so I suggested we get married. Maeve was dead set against it; she saw no need for it. I admired her for this view and supported it in one sense, but I was still of the opinion that it was one thing I could do to avoid my children having to put up with when they started school. So, with Maeve five months pregnant, we decided to get married in the Sydney Registry Office. We agreed that there would not be a church wedding for us.

Maeve bought a second-hand set of pink silk pyjamas for the wedding, something her rebellious self and feminist friends supported. She looked great. I had a suit jacket and trousers from when I was an office worker. We were married amongst friends and family in the Sydney Registry Office, then we went to Eve's house in Paddington where Maeve used to live for a post-wedding party. We had a great night. I danced most of the time with the American girlfriend of a friend of Maeve's, a teacher from New York, and enjoyed it immensely. Maeve didn't want to dance; she felt she was getting too heavy. She seemed to enjoy sitting and enjoying being pregnant and talking to friends, so I was fine with that.

Later, Maeve's father was at the kitchen table and I heard him say out loud so everyone could hear, "So where's that daughter of mine? Tell her to come here if she wants her present." He then presented Maeve with a cheque for $5000. A pittance considering what he was worth at the time. When Maeve told me how much the cheque was for, I replied, "Huh? What's that then? A ten per cent down payment?"

Our first son, Hugo, was born a healthy child after a short natural labour. He was beautiful. He had the whitest skin, blue eyes and a mass of bright red curls a tribute to his almost exclusively Celtic heritage. Of course, this is not the best skin for the Australian climate, but he has managed it well. He still remains clear-skinned and unblemished by the harsh climate and effects of the Australian sun that we of earlier less aware generations have to endure. What was important to me was that his facial features were unblemished, and he had all his fingers and toes. I checked.

After I was working for a while doing casual teaching in local schools and Hugo was in day care, Maeve was keen to have a second child. She began to be unwell and needed some time off work. She had a very difficult second pregnancy and by the time she stopped working to have the baby she was exhausted. The birth of our second child, Lenny, was difficult and he was a demanding baby for the first months of his life. By the time Maeve was due to return to work at the end of her maternity leave she was worn out. From then on, she was not a healthy person.

Our early life though, with both Maeve and I working as we did and the two kids in family day care, was hectic, busy and lots of fun. We were both earning reasonable money, so that wasn't a problem; we had money for the mortgage at 17½% interest and money to spend.

I was working at Minda Remand Centre, a penal institution for juveniles, in the girls' section. So much for my primary teaching training so that I could avoid teaching adolescents! I was locked in the same room as these tough adolescent girls at the start of the first period and the door was not opened until the morning recess break. The same routine repeated for the middle period. The girls were released for the lunch break and then again locked in for the afternoon period. I was at the mercy of the girls if they chose to play up, as they did on a number of occasions. In one incident I had a strong girl holding a heavy old typewriter over my head and threatening to drop it if I made a fuss about the other girls in the room rioting and throwing equipment around. I didn't; I just sat quietly and watched!

That was a pretty stressful work environment, but I was new and younger, so I had the energy for it. I was the father of two beautiful boys. Hugo and Lenny were both in day care and were happy, thriving and well looked after. Maeve was doing well at work and working longer hours than was good for her, travelling interstate to meetings, socialising with her colleagues, and overall managing admirably. I admired her enormously. But it was taking its toll on her health.

Eventually she collapsed and had some time off work. She went back again but soon relapsed and then announced she had decided to take a year off to try and improve her health. This was a disaster financially for us but there was little choice as it was evident to both of us that she had a debilitating illness. She was able to help with cooking and house care but her health didn't improve. Her lack of energy was a grave concern. I became more than full-time as I had to assume the great majority of childcare, housework, working to get an income and doing what I could to care for and make life easier for Maeve.

Chapter Thirty-Three

The Sole Breadwinner

Maeve was diagnosed with Chronic Fatigue Syndrome (CFS), or sometimes called Myalgic Encephalomyelitis (ME) in 1984. Some people who contract this recover, but Maeve never did. She was sent for many exploratory examinations and put on numerous experimental programs, but nothing changed or improved her condition. She was regularly in hospital, on various programs trying to find a treatment program that worked, diets, infusions, all in attempts to improve her health. She tried very boring diets of lettuce and boiled chicken breasts (and it was boring cooking this for her!). Overall there was nothing that improved her health enough that she could contemplate returning to work.

It was a great shame and such a disappointment for both of us. Maeve has spent these intervening years virtually as an invalid, unable to work, and in later years unable to socialise as she was used to and which she thrived on.

The kids have now grown and have their own lives, of course. Maeve is now in a nursing home. She copped a lot of flak from some medical people and others who suggested it was "all in her mind" when they couldn't find an explanation for her malaise. However, I knew that was not correct. She had a genuine and serious illness. We were both affected by the negative opinion of others.

For me, the disappointment revolved around having to assume so much of the financial burden and manage the day to day domestic work (though Maeve did assist there in a limited way). I lost an equal sharing relationship with a partner who could shoulder a good proportion of the load of living a full family life. It meant that life was always a struggle financially for us, and for me. It meant we didn't have the ready money to support other activities except household expenses. I wanted money to continue the renovations, buy the things we needed, continue my pottery and take the kids on family holidays. Instead, I needed to be mindful of other responsibilities in childcare, home duties and financial matters. I was always anxious that I had to keep working otherwise we would go backwards financially and not have enough to survive. I needed to continue working a couple of jobs to make enough money for our living needs. The constant demands of this situation grated on me over the years.

I worked as a casual teacher. After I was permanently appointed, I also got a night job as an adult migrant education teacher at the Adult Language Centre. That was interesting, but I stuck with teaching in schools as that was a permanent job. This meant I was always anxious about Maeve and about money. It also meant that any idea I had of exploring my sexuality further was put on hold, pushed aside and averted for even longer. Life was difficult, disappointing and frustrating.

One thing we did prioritise was the purchase of some land at Wollombi, about three hours north of Sydney in partnership with Maeve's sister, Eve, and brother-in-law, Hans. We did this because it seemed that we would not ever have the money, or Maeve the health, to travel. Since we lived in the inner city, we wanted the kids to have an experience of life in the country as we had had.

This also allowed me to get back to the country. It was a beautiful, isolated environment. I loved the isolation, the rocks, trees, hills, creeks and the bush. There were lots of bush wombats and other native animals. It was beautiful, peaceful country, and I loved it. Sometimes I would go there by myself and enjoy the peacefulness of the bush. Knowing the attraction I had for the place stopped me fretting about not facing up to my sexuality. Many times, we would go there as a family and it was great to see my kids relaxed and to facilitate their enjoyment of the place. We had a rustic, roomy cabin built, with a huge fireplace at one end. We loved camping there as a family. One of the downsides was that I spent a lot of time mowing the area around the cabin to keep the grass and scrub down. But we did have some wonderful times there.

Eventually though, soon after we sold it, the cabin was burnt down by a bushfire. Such a shame. But it was a beautiful, relaxing, fun, space for us for the short time we had it.

Meanwhile I was also renovating the house at Darlington; and that took money! I loved that old house. We lived with the characteristic uneven plastered walls and ceilings, with finger marks in the bricks that had been made by hand.

Maeve's health continued to slowly decline. She always wanted to get better enough so she could return to work but none of the treatments worked well enough to make any noticeable difference. It seemed any treatment, trial, or program she tried showed no worthwhile improvement and only wore her out even more. Meanwhile life with work and the kids continued apace.

I've been asked if Maeve told me how much she appreciated my input and my concern for her at the time. I don't think she ever did in as many words. She knew how much I cared and did for her and appreciated my concern and support, but she showed this in other ways. She helped when she could by participating in trips and outings, trying to do her bit with the kids and in the home, even though it was a huge effort for her. I felt a lot of compassion for her; her life was a great disappointment for both of us.

I was active in the Movement Against Uranium Mining (MAUM) and if Maeve was well enough, she would come with me. We would go to the rallies in town with the kids. I liked that we were still able to be active politically and encouraged Maeve to continue to participate if she were well enough.

During this time, I completely built the bathroom upstairs, suspending it between the two walls of the existing house. I was proud of this effort. It became one of my distinguished renovation projects! I painted, renovated and renewed the kitchen and continued renovating the whole house.

We spent many weekends at the land at Laguna, enjoying the bush and the change of pace. My awareness was aroused by faint tracks I discerned along the base of the rocks and through the bush, as if other quiet people had been here many times before me. With the kids' help we built a track up the hill that followed these barely discernible steps. It was a beautiful bush area around our house at Laguna, and it was easy to feel that others had passed this way over the years.

My life seemed to be working well, I was very busy all the time and, on purpose, had little time to reflect. However, the old anxiety about money and needing more was always in the background.

Maeve knew how busy my life was and where I was at any time. It was a predictable and routine life, so I had no time to myself that I could feel free to do my own thing. I began to feel frustrated and yearn for my own time without this constant feeling I was being watched. Not that I blamed Maeve; she wasn't intentionally watching me, only that I knew she would be aware that I was not doing what I was supposed to be doing if I was off doing something else. If I was late home from work or didn't show up when I had said I would, she knew. She would want to know where I'd been.

In the last term of the year in 1984 I was relieved from my role at Minda School and seconded to a program designed to support Community Care Schools of which Minda was one. I was based in the city, and this meant I could organise a couple of hours of time that I could be free of accounting for my time.

I used one afternoon to go to a gay bathhouse in the city I had heard about, where I was free to indulge myself. It was a great experience, one that I wasn't able to repeat for another twelve years of restraint, but it showed me that I did indeed enjoy the company of men, and that I could respond more than adequately to a sexual experience with them. I found it more satisfying than I ever would have expected. I felt relieved and whole in some strange way and glad I'd had the experience. Then I returned to my life of abstinence. However, the fact that I did not indulge in any untoward gay activity for another twelve years shows the level of restraint and inhibition I placed on myself.

I returned to my commitment to Maeve and my family. I did what I had to do to support them, living my life of work, weekends at Laguna, renovating the house and being a good father, husband, family member, neighbour and productive member of the workforce.

I was also developing my interest in pottery and working with clay. I had done a couple of classes at uni and then continued to hand-build clay vessels at home. Eventually, I was able to afford a second-hand kiln, which I rebuilt and began firing in a studio shed I built in the backyard at Darlington. That was a great achievement, and I had a lot of satisfaction in unloading kiln loads of my own work. I had also bought a second-hand pottery wheel so began making my own hand turned pots and firing them at home. Selling it to people who admired it was also a buzz. The greatest buzz was walking into a friend's house who had bought some pieces and seeing how much they enjoyed them.

I sold them at the local markets in company with another colleague who was also a potter. It was fun, and I enjoyed the creative outlet. It was another way of being at home and being an attentive father and partner meanwhile distracting myself from discomforting thoughts.

My time at Minda ended with the Community Care Program, and I was accepted into the Special Education Certificate course at Ku-Ring-Gai College. This was a great respite year of being a student again. A two-year stint at a special school in Croydon followed where I passed my first inspection to get qualifications to be promoted.

At the end of 1987 I was transferred to relieve as principal at Clairvaux Special School in Katoomba. I didn't know much about Clairvaux except it was a school for emotionally disturbed children, but we needed the money and it was a small step in promotion, so I put my hand up for the job. I didn't have anyone to ask and get a lay of the land, so I jumped in head first. Big mistake.

It was a horror show from the beginning, and I was totally unprepared for what I was expected to cope with in the position. I was traumatised from the first, and I reacted as I always did. It brought up all my trauma from the past, and I shut down and withdrew. For the first several months I did not adequately lead the staff and support them in the demands of the work with these damaged students. Often, I felt unable to adequately respond in a constructive manner to the behaviour I was confronted with; I withdrew from exposure to the students. No matter how much I wanted it otherwise, I could not cope with the students at the school. I was fortunate that some of the staff were more than capable, and I relied heavily on their expertise to get me through each day. I am forever grateful for their support.

As it turned out the school only remained open for eighteen months, although we were not told it was to close when I started. At this distance, I harbour some anger toward the Education Department and its representatives for putting me in that position. I had no idea it would be so challenging and that the school was going through a period of winding down. I was personally challenged with my own trauma as well. I received no support or recognition of this except from the staff that had to cope with my response to trauma as well as the behaviour of the students.

Clairvaux was a collection of old institutional buildings near the clifftops of the Jamieson Valley. I experienced a distinct feeling of dread whenever I was there. I believe this had to do with the treatment of the indigenous inhabitants in earlier years. I could feel their presence, their terror. These precipitous cliffs would have been ideal to drive the indigenous inhabitants off the edge to plunge to their deaths. What I gleaned of the history of this area confirmed what the basis of these feelings of dread were a result of. It was a dark place, heavy with negative energy.

Chapter Thirty-Four

New Challenges

When Clairvaux closed in mid-1989, I transferred to a local regular primary school as I wanted a "normal" school to work at. Again, this was another difficult school to work at, especially after Clairvaux. I was appointed assistant principal of the school. The principal was on the verge of retiring and not at all interested in running the school, so all the expectations and responsibilities of ensuring the school functioned appropriately were delegated to me. With the demands of my domestic situation and of work, I felt I was running backwards.

One of the new staff was a male teacher about my age, married, very artistic and creative, and a musician. He was great to have onside and we helped each other organise activities to entertain, have fun and instruct the students. He was a great ally. For example, we would decide together if we would both wear bow-ties to school the next day and give the students something to talk about and be stimulated by.

I found working with him so uplifting. Hurrying to get organised one morning I was walking with him down to the office, laughing and talking excitedly about what we were doing that day. Suddenly I found myself saying to him "Because I love you." I gave myself a big fright as I had to swallow these words, but it was obvious to me that I did love him. I was vulnerable to loving another man and in fact I wanted to, my heart wanted to. He ended up transferring to another school soon after, and I felt disconsolate when he left.

I was drawn to a parent of one of my students. I would see him walking around the playground waiting for his children to get out of school. Ralph was a mature age student at the time. I admired him. He was a tall, slim, good-looking man of German background, very gentle and easy to talk to. I fantasised about falling in love with him but that was not on; he was a parent and straight, so that would not do. I remained friendly with him as a parent of the school and met him again a few years later when I joined a men's therapy group.

During this time, I was a DJ on a program on Saturday night from 9:00 p.m. to midnight, the quiet time, at the local community radio station, Blue Mountains Community Radio. I used to go in with my load of vinyl Long Plays and sit in this little booth playing my records and talking to the ether; to anyone who listened. I don't think I ever knew if anyone did ever listen but I didn't care. I had a great time.

My program was called *Women Who Rock,* and I played my favourite rocking women and their music. Chryssie Amphlett and the Divinyls, Chrissie Hinds and the Pretenders, Tina Turner, Cher, Bonnie Tyler, Janis Joplin, LaBelle, The Supremes and many others were favourites. Great 80's and 90's rocking women. I wonder why it was women I liked to play more than male performers? I enjoyed this little solitary chance of hiding away and grooving to my favourite music.

After I had spent a few years at this Upper Blue Mountains school in a promotions position it was the end of term school holidays. It was January 1990. Feeling depressed about my work and life prospects, I was walking with my sons and our friend's kids at their place on the Central Coast, north of Sydney. As I walked across a narrow ledge on a rock face, I found myself suddenly sliding down the face of the rock. This was unusual because I was always very nimble on rocks and steep hills. I thought I must have momentarily blacked out.

A few days later I went to the GP and he sent me for a CT scan. I knew there was something amiss when after one scan through the machine I was suddenly surrounded by doctors and nursing staff asking in a concerned fashion if I was okay. Had I suffered a stroke lately? Or a head injury? They sent me home and I saw my GP. After a two-week delay, I was admitted to Westmead Hospital.

I was diagnosed with Hydrocephaly. It transpired I had a huge epidermoid cyst growing in my skull. It had been growing so long my skull at the back had been worn away to the thickness of an eggshell. I spent thirty days in hospital having exploratory surgery and a shunt inserted to drain the cystic fluid matter. I later had the shunt closed off. This has also meant that I have to go to hospital for a repeat operation every six to eight years to have the cyst drained when it has regrown.

Recuperating from this trauma and not knowing if this could return as a life-threatening condition, I decided I needed to get my head in order, so I started meditation at a Buddhist temple in Katoomba. This helped me stay calm, gave me some tools to focus and centre myself, and helped me strengthen myself mentally. I continued to attend the temple regularly for many months, and stayed connected to it for several years, meditating, attending retreats and doing tasks around the temple. I never felt that a life of a monk was for me, but it did give me a solid background in meditation and the benefits of meditation. I still intermittently practise this today.

I enjoyed running on the walking tracks of the escarpment at Wentworth Falls. The running kept me fit and helped me avoid thinking about my issues. Meditation, combined with yoga and other physical exercise such as running, swimming or riding my pushbike have been so benificial to me over the years in coping with the vicissitudes of life, in dealing with my anxiety and depression and in assisting me to keep a positive attitude.

Around this time Maeve and I became interested in Reiki. I looked on Reiki as another avenue of spiritual growth. Reiki is like an energy transference through your hands. I did Reiki 1 and Reiki 2 and became quite adept at at using Reiki as a form of healing of muscular discomfort and treating illness.

I used to go to a Reiki group in the Blue Mountains where we would transfer Reiki to each other. That was very special. I tried it on Maeve several times but with little relief reported. I once offered a colleague who had severe back pain a Reiki session to try and relieve her discomfort. I gave her a session of "hands on" Reiki one afternoon and she reported considerable relief. She could then stand up straight and walk without pain. I was pleased with that but unfortunately Reiki was not something I continued with. Other things got in the way. However I have recently returned to using the symbols on myself with noticeable results.

Towards the end of 1990 I took some long service leave and went on a trek in Nepal. I needed to get away and take a break from work for my health after the surgery as well as give myself a break from this constant urge to do something about my sexuality. I had the leave and the couple of thousand dollars I needed to pay for it. I joined an Australian Expeditions group and went on a twenty-nine-day trek through western Nepal and into the remote Dolpo region. It was wonderful, remarkable, exhausting and challenging. We trekked over about seven high passes, camped in snow above the snowline, trekked through picturesque villages, gazed at mountain passes. I loved it. Every step was another step away from the difficulties of the life I was leaving behind. I loved the challenge, the isolation, the mountains and the terrain, the people. It was an exhilarating and different holiday experience.

It was an emotional journey as well. Several times I became quite emotional and excused it as the physical demands of the trek; but I knew it was also the unrelenting anxiety, fear and implications of the of the feelings I carried with me. Feelings I wanted to trek away from. To leave behind. Every step, every mountain pass, was a step and a pass away from what I was leaving behind. Yet it was all still there, waiting for me to deal with it.

Chapter Thirty-Five

The Loss of What Never Was

I returned to work at the primary school, and Dad died soon after. By the early 90's, he had been increasingly difficult for Mum to live with. She managed, as she always had, but at times Dad was drinking far too much, his behaviour was unpredictable, he was frequently morose and unhappy. His health was deteriorating, and he had a number of heart attacks that involved hospital. He had a triple by-pass and seemed to improve for a while after that. But his drinking continued. And he was frequently in hospital for further tests or recovery. The untreated PTSD from his war experiences was really affecting his mental and physical health.

Dad was back in hospital after yet another heart attack. I had been to see him in the hospital the previous night. He looked pathetic, drained, unhappy. He just lay there and looked at me occasionally, but mostly looked away. We had some inconsequential and desultory talk; all I could ever expect from Dad. It was too difficult trying to broach anything of substance with him and besides, he was in a very low state. As I was leaving, he handed me a small bag of washing to "take to Mum." I wasn't going home that way, but I took it anyway. I would do it at home. As I said goodbye and was leaving his bedside he just looked away and didn't respond or say anything. I didn't even kiss his cheek. No goodbye, no acknowledgement.

At work the next day I got summoned from class to the office for an "urgent" phone call. It was Maeve telling me Dad had died. I immediately just collapsed in the office; I was howling and helpless. At the same time, I was amazed at my reaction. It was like I was watching myself, howling loudly and grieving. It unleashed years of a frustrating lack of communication and the loss of the opportunity to have any meaningful relationship with my father.

At his funeral later that week I sat in the front pew and looked across at his coffin, not feeling anything very much really, maybe it was a quietness, a numbness, a sadness I was feeling. I saw him floating, reclining and peaceful, above his coffin, looking down at the congregation gathered on his behalf. He looked at peace and quietly enjoying being the reason for people to be there, but I sensed he seemed pleased he was no longer part of this life. It was a good feeling in a way; it provided me some peace and closure, something to comfort my heart, my sadness and loss.

However, trust Mum to put things off; stoic to the end. She had finally gone into hospital on the morning Dad died for a gall-bladder operation she had put off and put off. When the surgeon opened up her stomach cavity, as he told us later, he saw that the gall-bladder had in fact burst some time before, that it was cancerous, and the cancer had spread throughout her stomach cavity. So, he just sewed her up and discharged her. Mum went home and resumed her normal life. What a shock it was for her, and us, to find out she had incurable cancer on the same morning her husband of forty-seven years died.

Soon after I was accepted into the two-year School Counsellor Training course at Charles Sturt University.

I saw this as an alternative to the "running backwards" I felt was happening with my current job. This post-graduate degree was difficult work, a lot of it research and essay writing, but after the experiences I had had at Clairvaux and North Katoomba, I welcomed it. And I was paid a normal salary, so home finances remained the same. It also meant that I could use this degree to qualify as a registered psychologist.

Chapter Thirty-Six

The Loss of What Always Is

Mum had nursed several friends and neighbours through death by cancer, and she immediately announced that she was not going to go down the radiation and chemotherapy route. Prolonged death was not for her. It was a definite decision that we respected. That was it for her as far as she was concerned. She was not yet sixty-nine; too young.

In recent months we had discussed the fact that Dad's death seemed imminent. We imagined that with him gone and Mum still a healthy sixty-eight-year-old, she would have at least a decade of life to travel and enjoy her family and grandchildren, free of the demands of a difficult partner. Not to be.

The twelve months after Dad's death were spent wondering when Mum's time would come. For most of that time Mum was pretty healthy and active, still visiting her old friends, active with the church, doing the flowers for the altar. But the clock was ticking. Eventually she began to crumble, and it was amazing how quickly she lost weight and became a frail and thin old person, a shell of her former self. Still the Mum we loved but rapidly fading.

I was back at uni again studying for the post-graduate counselling degree to become a school counsellor. My education took a back seat to caring for Mum. I remember being in an exam and not being able to concentrate on the questions because I was thinking of Mum's imminent departure. Bill, Maree, Alice and I decided we would care for Mum at home, which is what she wanted and the four of us were happy to do.

My family was living in Wentworth Falls in the Blue Mountains. My routine became going to uni during the day, then to Mum's to do a shift of caring for her, then home. Sometimes I was able to stay over at Mum's if I didn't have uni work the next day. Other times I would go to uni, go home to see Maeve and the kids, do what I had to do and then drive down the hill to Mum's and move into my hours of caring for her.

I really enjoyed those final days and weeks with Mum and cherish the times I had sitting with her, doing her hair, caring for her. Talking if she wanted to. Once I was doing the night shift, about two in the morning; it was so quiet, the house was sleeping. She was sitting on the bed, this tiny, frail woman who was my mother, by this time a shadow of her former self. We were both quiet and peaceful and I was gently brushing her hair. Suddenly she quietly looked up at me and asked, "Tony, do you think I'm a bludger?" Those words knocked me sideways at the time — Mum, a bludger! I just laughed and told her "No, of course you're not a bludger." She had been the hardest working person I knew. That just encapsulated to me what sort of values and principles she lived her life by. She had worked hard all her life, did her best to make ends meet, and see that her husband and her eight kids were loved and well cared for. Definitely not my idea of a bludger.

It was a beautiful time and we all felt the same. I know my other four brothers loved Mum as much as we did, but they spent as little time as possible in her company. We were all fortunate to be with Mum as she breathed the final laboured breaths of her fading life. We controlled her medication and when we thought she needed it we increased it a small bit. Mum had been semi-comatose for several days and we continued to tend to her. This was three days before Christmas and Mum had lasted until now to keep us together for an occasion that meant so much to her.

Around midday we sensed a change in her breathing and slowly that afternoon her breathing became shallower and shallower. Luckily, all of her children and her sister, Aunty Peg, were with her that afternoon. I was holding her head and softly talking to her, gently telling her that she was free to go. Finally, she took a deep sighing exhale, then a long pause and then another shallow breath and then she was gone. Gently, like letting go, with great relief.

I like to think I sensed her leave her body, a body she had no further use for. But I felt she was still strongly present in the room. It was a beautiful way for Mum to finish, and for us all to be there to share this moment.

Later we sat around Mum, reminiscing into the night, and finally agreed that we should call the undertakers to take the body. I waited in the room with Mum for the undertakers to arrive. It seemed to me then that this form I saw before me was just like a dead tree; it had lived its life and was now returning to the earth, as decaying trees do. Whereas the energy who was Mum, who had given this body life, was returning to meld with the Universal Energy of the cosmos. Mum was still with us, with me. This body may not be Mum anymore, but Mum was strongly present in this space, strongly with me in the room as I waited with her discarded body. I watched impassively as the undertakers simply bundled this dry crust into the body bag, zipped it shut and carried it to the hearse outside. I knew I could be impassive as I watched her body being removed, as

I knew that Mum was still with me, and us, and she remains so. I still take comfort that Mum has returned to the energy of the cosmos and so for me is still here.

For all the time I was growing up there was a pink pelargonium growing beside the steps at the back door. Mum's pelargonium. I had taken a cutting from it years before and grew it beside the door at my family home. Over the years I have grown cuttings of this pelargonium and taken them with me as I have moved. I still have them growing and love the brilliant pink blossoms. To me they are Mum's pelargoniums, a reminder of her presence. Recognising Mum is with me.

Chapter Thirty-Seven

Travelling North

During this time both Maeve and I became enamoured of a Californian spiritual guru, Gangaji, who came to Australia for spiritual retreats. Her understanding of the human condition was very helpful and insightful. Her followers hosted retreats in Sydney and the North Coast of NSW, which I attended as far as time and money would allow.

On one occasion there was a spiritual retreat being held at Byron Bay. It required driving to the far North Coast and camping. I was keen to attend. Maeve regretfully didn't feel she could easily cope with the driving and the camping, so we agreed for me to go alone for the weekend retreat (which was all we could afford).

So, leaving Maeve and the kids behind in the Blue Mountains, I headed north. To limit costs, I packed the tent and sleeping bag, some clothes and food and a small single burner stove fired by a gas cartridge, and off I went. I left after work on Thursday and planned to drive several hours and camp for the night. There is something soothing and liberating about driving a great distance alone at night. I love the sense of freedom it gives. I can legitimately be alone, no one can contact me (before the time of cell phones), no responsibilities except to drive safely and arrive back home to resume family life. I was looking forward to spending time absorbing Gangaji's wisdom, her words, her strength, energy, presence and the spiritual connection. Beautiful.

By the time I neared Port Macquarie it started to rain. Hoping it might ease, I kept driving. By the time I got near Nambucca Heads it was pitch black and raining so heavily I could hardly see. Too wet for camping.

I knew of a cheaper motel near Nambucca that Maeve and I and the kids had stayed at several times, so I pulled in there to see if there was a vacancy. The only bed left was a single room right beside the office; imagine a poky little room with no outside window and hence no ventilation. Though I always felt claustrophobic with no fresh air flow, I decided that this was worth it if the alternative was a wet night in a tent — if I could even find somewhere to camp at this time of night.

The sign said: "No Cooking in Rooms." But I had a minimum of money to last the weekend and had brought food to eat, so heating it on the little gas camping stove seemed a good option. A bit risky perhaps but should be fine. Besides it was still pouring outside and where would I find something to eat at this time of night?

The room was so cramped as I began to set up the little gas stove on the floor. It was one of the types where the gas cartridge had to be clipped into the burner by a clamp that pierced the membrane of the cartridge and sealed it to the burner. I had used these many times on camping trips, so I felt fairly confident. However, this unit was borrowed from a friend and I hadn't used it before.

Trying to set it up was a bit tricky because it all had to happen at once. Low and behold the clamp pierced the cartridge OK but failed to clamp the cartridge into the stove securely. Suddenly there was gas hissing away like a smelly-breathed, combustible, stinking and noisy viper.

Ack! What to do? Stay calm! Stay calm!

I had to subdue my panic. I was terrified that it would explode or that the manager would smell it and cause a scene! How was I to quiet this violently hissing cartridge, get it out of the room and disposed of without the manager catching on? How to get this screaming monster bundled up and safely away from the people smoking outside under the veranda without it exploding and without anyone seeing me or smelling the gas! Oh, why did I think I could heat my food?

A frantic search for something to seal the cartridge in like a container was fruitless. Where's a Tupperware container when you need one? Nothing was there. In an extremely heightened state of focussed panic I did the only thing that came to hand: I frantically wrapped the thrashing monster in a towel, opened the door and bundled myself past the smokers and into the car. "Stay calm," I kept repeating to myself, trying to breath in a controlled way.

With great relief, I left the motel behind. I drove out on to the highway in the still teeming rain. What to do now? I drove up to the edge of town hoping to see a park or a rubbish bin but in the dark and the rain I didn't have any luck. Just lots of rain, lots of darkness, lots of traffic and reflecting lights feeling their way through the rain. Eventually, there was nothing for it. Pulling over to the edge of the road I leaned across and tried to throw the cartridge into the culvert out of the passenger side door. The dastardly hissing monster hit the edge of the car door and rolled under the car! I leaned out and saw it was illuminated by the cars behind me, hissing away under my car.

I frantically leaned across the seats, scrambled around under the car and located the cartridge. I tried to toss it as far as I could into the grass. The damned monster went about a foot. It was still hissing gas in the car lights behind me. Nothing for it; I left it there, hissing its betrayal into the rain and darkness and drove off.

Back at the motel, no one seemed any the wiser. I went to bed hungry but hardly slept. This was not a conducive beginning to my spiritual retreat.

Chapter Thirty-Eight

This Is Not My Coming Out

It was 1994 and our son Hugo was 15. He came out and told Maeve and I that he was gay. Maeve and I had talked about the possibility between ourselves and felt it was likely the case. His actions up to then, his behaviour and way of acting, reminded us of the friends we had who were gay. We had already decided we knew so it was no surprise, but we were proud that he had been able to tell us straight out without fear that he would be negatively judged.

Anyway, he was ready and he told us his thoughts and decisions. That was all fine by us and we were both very supportive. Our only concern was that he would be okay at school. He had experienced some severe bullying at high school, both from the students and as we found out, by a staff member. By the time he came out to us we had enrolled him at a small alternative school, which we expected would be much more supportive. It was great to see the relief in Hugo as he relaxed into the new role he had accepted for himself. My son had accepted himself but what did this say to me about not having made my decision before this and still being in an anxious dilemma of indecision?

Hugo asked us about attending an ACON (a gay support organisation) course for young men just coming out. We were supportive of this, however it meant me collecting him after work then driving him down to Oxford Street in the city to the ACON offices — a 100 kilometre/90+-minute drive. He would go to the group himself, and I'd pick him up afterwards. This was a big ask for me, but I was happy to do it for him. I wanted to support him any way I could.

I found myself dropping Hugo — my son, a beautiful red-headed boy — off in the wilds of Oxford street and letting him go alone for several hours. During the time he was in the group I was at a loose end and I wandered around Oxford Street wondering what to do. I didn't feel I could just go to a sauna but that I had to be a responsible parent, so I didn't indulge. I was too anxious to in any case. I would pick him up in Oxford Street at the appointed time and drive the 100 kilometres home with this brave son of mine next to me. Hugo was facing his world and I was still firmly in the closet. My son had come out before me. It was becoming glaringly obvious to me that I would have to make a decision and come out for myself sometime in the not too distant future; I just didn't know when, or how.

After I had graduated as a school counsellor, I was appointed to a school in the far western suburbs of Sydney, on the western plains near Penrith. This was fine and, after a while, routine, but it meant I had a fifty-kilometre commute from home to there and back every day. This gave me some freedom to organise my time and not be so predictable. The kids were getting older as well and had become more independent in travelling.

I spent about seven years working there as the school counsellor at that school and other schools in my "patch." It became quite mundane after a while, but

I enjoyed it and I enjoyed the group of colleagues in my counselling group. They were a good, supportive and "collegial" group, some of whom I became good friends with.

During the mid to late 90's I joined a men's weekly therapy group in Katoomba. I was studying psychology but had never engaged in any therapy myself up until then, so it seemed like a good thing to experience. It was run by a therapist I had seen a couple of times just before I joined the group. The group consisted of about seven men, one of whom was Ralph, the parent of the student in my class at school. The group was to run for a year, but I became quite disillusioned with the format of the group. I felt the co-ordinator should or could have provided some direction to the discussion. As it happened, discussion was up to the participants and seemed to consist of several of them complaining about their lot, their life, their relationship with their partner or their children. I found myself withdrawing from participating in the discussion; my mind was somewhere else.

I was again going through a lot of anxiety and doubt about my sexuality. I still had not come out, and I regret not feeling safe enough with them to take them into my confidence. We did, however, have a couple of times where we stayed as a group and had some interesting activities like building a "Heat Dome" with blankets and hot stones, and a weekend of "Re-birthing." Both were excellent activities and opened me up to alternate ways of engaging in the therapeutic process. After both these activities I felt "released" in some way — relaxed. We continued to meet for some considerable time after the end of the group and the therapist departed. This was less about the complaints of the participants and more about current issues.

After an intense period of fulfilling the requirements for registration, I was fully registered as a psychologist in 1998. This also meant that I was able to take on some private clients, which I enjoyed. It also helped make ends meet and extend my professional life.

In the early 1990's I had renewed my friendship with Peter Rushforth, the eminent Australian Potter, through Maeve and the OzCo, and he graciously invited me to work with him at his studio and help out with firings and sales. I was very honoured and over several years spent many mornings and afternoons working alongside him. It was very generous of him, and I felt quite honoured to be there with the great master. He was such a modest man. My work improved enormously in that time, and I still have many pots from that period. Others who bought my work from then also say it was a very good period for my work.

Not long before I left primary school in the west of Sydney to move to the inner city, an incident occurred that marred my pleasant memories I had of the school. I was in a planning meeting with the principal and a couple of other staff and the topic of playground duty came up. As counsellor I was exempt from playground duty. However, the issue of staff time to put into the project was being discussed and the principal suddenly turned on me and ridiculed me for not helping out with playground duty and relying on other staff to cover for me. I was appalled at being spoken to and criticised like that in front of other staff. I tried to protect myself but was vindictively put down and my comments dismissed by the principal. I tried to respond to his unfounded accusations at the time, but my voice was strangled by my body and my psyche's response to the suddenness of his attack on me. I was speechless at his ferocity; obviously this was a product of frustration with the system and his own job. My relationship with him from then on was very tricky, and as with the unpredictability of my father, I was very wary of him. My response to trauma of fear and shutting down arose, and I was not able to interact with him again at a professional level. I knew he was under stress but his behaviour toward me was very unprofessional.

During my time at the school in Western Sydney I noticed I had this ringing noise in my ears. I talked to other staff members about this, and they figured I had tinnitus; I'd never heard of it. I tried various remedies they suggested, but nothing made any difference, nor has since. I have never had a break from it since that time. I have never had any luck with ameliorating the noise in my head either. It's something I have had to learn to manage.

I have struggled to cope with it. Each time I mention tinnitus to a medical person or anyone else, they don't hear it, or they roll their eyes, change the subject or simply ignore it. No one ever says, "What is it like?" or "How loud or disruptive or distracting is it?" Tinnitus is one of those bloody ailments that simply will not ever go away yet has such an effect on every waking and sleeping moment. I know it is affected by stress levels and certainly by anxiety. When these are low and I am feeling relaxed the tinnitus is more manageable; when I am stressed or depressed or feeling anxious it is barely bearable.

It seems that the medical profession has no remedy or treatment for it; it is something they can't assist with. I tried Cognitive Behaviour Therapy (CBT) on the recommendation of a psychologist at the hearing clinic but to no effect. CBT was hopeless. The sound card works to some degree to help me to get to sleep. The bloody burden of it is that it is there all the time — all the time, never a break. I'm always carrying this distracting and disabling noise everywhere, every waking moment.

It affects everything. Trying to sit quietly or heaven forbid, to meditate is very difficult.

It's there now, a huge, dominating buzzing in my head. Never lets up. Never a break.

Chapter Thirty-Nine

Going Nowhere

Though I believe I still loved Maeve, I was fed up with my relationship, my sex life was very uninspired and unrewarding, my life was one of routine and tedium, and I had to deal with this constant urge to involve myself with men either sexually and/or emotionally. It was an urge that was making me extremely anxious about the consequences for Maeve and my family, as much as I wished it were otherwise.

People comment that I must not have loved Maeve during this time, but that is a mistake. I did love Maeve and still do many years later. I was trying to deal with that love and what it should mean, and the fact that I was contemplating something I knew was destructive, hurtful and unfair to her. It is a decision faced by many men going through this transition, but, unfortunately, it had to happen, much as I regret having to do it to Maeve.

One day I arranged to meet this guy at a pub in Springwood on the way home. We did, it was easy, and I felt fine. I was having increasing difficulty ignoring and denying the thoughts I was having. We chatted and had a beer and agreed to meet at his house on an afternoon soon after, which we did. Interestingly, he had a huge, partly swollen cock, which to my untrained eye, looked like he had had an implant that didn't seem to be working particularly well. He couldn't have sex (just my luck) but seemed happy to give me a hand job. This was sort of fine for me, but I managed with hand jobs myself and someone else giving me one was not all that exciting.

One afternoon soon after, he was masturbating me, and I got a severe shooting headache. It was weird and off-putting, but very like headaches I had had before that indicated a build of the cystic fluid in my skull. I went to the GP, and he sent me for another CT scan. I again had a build-up of fluid in my head, a return of my previous condition. This required another stint in hospital to drain the cyst that just kept growing. It was also an excuse that put an end to that little escape hatch.

In the winter holidays, Maeve and I went south to her relatives on the farm at Henty and then to Albury to see her parents. The kids stayed behind with friends, so it was just the two of us. It was a pleasant enough holiday and we got on well, but we didn't have sex at all, and I didn't try to initiate any. A night or two after we arrived home, still having had no sex, Maeve asked me, "Are you okay?" meaning "We haven't had sex for a while."

I replied, "Yes, I'm okay but I've got something to tell you. I've been having sex with a man."

Of course, she was flabbergasted and upset. She wanted to know who it was, how long, how many? Of course, I didn't have any answers for her, and we eventually slept. The next morning, she was very emotional and upset. I didn't want to continue to upset her, so I lied and said I wouldn't do it again. I told her I'd "be happy to stay living with you." I didn't feel good about lying but didn't know what else to say.

We went to a counsellor several times, but I knew that in the long-term it wouldn't help. Eventually, I would want to split with her and come out as a gay man. I knew it was devastating for her, but I felt that I was on a path that I wanted to be on and, really, I didn't have any choice. My heart bled for her because of the emotional and physical condition she was in, but I knew I did not want this relationship to continue. We returned to our previous life and arrangements, and I withdrew into my shell again; I involved myself yet again with the heterosexual life of a married man. However, this time I knew my time was not unlimited.

I went on a ten-day silent meditation retreat to get away from it all: the thoughts in my head, the demands of my body. It was great and I really enjoyed it, but it didn't provide any answers, any solutions, any alternatives. Still the demands of my body were paramount.

Maeve and I stayed this way for several more years, and I sank into the routine of life. I remember thinking that this would be the last time I painted the house, something I wouldn't be around to repeat. I was working on my pottery with Peter Rushforth, running after work along the walking tracks around the escarpment. This helped me let off steam and deal with the constant urges that just kept arising.

My intention was that before I did anything, I would wait for both the kids to leave high school. Eventually, the time came that Hugo was in Melbourne studying and Lenny had finished Year 12 the year before and was enjoying a "gap" year. I had been feeling depressed and moody for weeks and despondent about work, but really it was about what I needed to resolve, and that the implications of what I was feeling were inevitable for my kids, for Maeve, for me.

Maeve said to me one afternoon after work, "You've been really moody for weeks; you need to talk about what's bugging you."

It was an invitation that almost said to me that she knew what was behind my depression, silence and moodiness.

I said, "I know. I do want to talk about it. But not now. I will soon." And left it at that. All that week I knew something was about to change. That my offer to talk "soon" would mean that it would have irrevocable consequences when it happened. I went through that week at work, shopping, cooking, dealing with the daily routines. I was actually floating on a cloud. It was like something had broken. Like I had taken a step into the abyss. Like I was not going to go back. I felt my heart hardening against the concerns I felt for Maeve and how she would be affected by it. My heart was telling me it was now or never. That Friday afternoon we were taking the dog for a walk up the road, something we often did and about as far as Maeve was able to walk.

I said to Maeve, "Okay, we've got some time to talk so let's talk." And once I started, I knew that life would never be the same.

So, I talked. It all came tumbling out. I said I could not remain in the relationship any longer. That I had to address what it was that had been affecting me for all these years. That I needed to explore my yearnings for the company of men. That I had remained generally faithful to her all these years; if not entirely physically but certainly emotionally. That I wasn't leaving her for another man or a lover. That yes, I had had some experience but that was very limited and infrequent. That I had waited for the kids to leave high school before I acted on this. That my allegiances were still with her and the kids.

I told her that I was unhappy and depressed at how I was feeling. That I wanted to have sex and intimate relations with men. That I didn't see any future for our relationship. That I needed to do something positive about how I felt. That I had been having these thoughts for years and now they were getting unbearable. I told her that it wasn't that I didn't love her, but that I needed the company of a man now.

Chapter Forty

Never Going Back

By the end of that walk with the dog I knew there was no going back. My marriage to Maeve was over. I felt such relief that I had finally been able to say how I felt and how I was suffering. There wasn't anything I could do anymore; I had tried.

It broke her heart, but I also expected she would have some understanding of my predicament, having had a gay brother, gay friends and a gay son. But no. Maeve was devastated, emotional and angry.

As it was, I was only too pleased to be out of it. I was on cloud nine. After about two weeks Maeve demanded that I leave the house as she couldn't stand the smugness I was displaying. It wasn't smugness. It was relief. I had finally made a decision and "come out." I had finally acted on what had kept me anxious and depressed all these years. We began a separation very soon after. It was mid-2000 when I left the marriage and moved into my life as a single gay man.

I knew Maeve would have to go on the disability pension, which was as a real slap in the face for her dignity. She could not afford to buy her own house, she had no income, she wouldn't get a mortgage; she had lived a middle-class life devoid of any reliance on welfare. I thought the only fair thing would be to give her the house so long as I got to keep the superannuation, which we arranged. She was, understandably, constantly emotional and needy at this time. She wanted a car like the one we had, so I also used the last $10,000 from Mum's estate that I had saved for a trip overseas to buy her a car like mine that she was confident she could drive. I spent the next couple of years in the Blue Mountains and tried to get on my feet financially but with little success. I did though enjoy my own company at my rented house at Lawson, the company of a few gay men I met and working on the plains of Western Sydney.

I had left the marital home with no house, no deposit to try and buy another one for myself, no money in the bank, and I was back to paying rent. I was also supporting Hugo as he was studying at Victorian College of the Arts in Melbourne. This short-sighted generosity made from guilt and compassion for Maeve, resulted in years of frustration and disappointment for me as I have struggled to get enough money for another house for myself. If I had insisted on say $30,000 from the house when I left, I would not have had to struggle ever since to get the deposit for a house. At that time $30,000 was enough for a deposit on a small cottage in the Blue Mountains. I would have been on the way. But not to be.

These decisions, made through guilt towards Maeve, have affected my financial life and sense of security ever since. I would not have ended up in the unmanageable debt I incurred with others when trying to invest in property if I wasn't trying to fast track my plans. If I had a small house I was paying off I would not have been tempted to go into risky debt. I would not be in the situation that I am in at present, living in my partner's house and not having a share in it. I have difficulty in dealing with the insecurity of not owning a house anymore, with no real prospect of owning a reasonable one. It was always important to me to own, and I achieved this over the years. I would not have had to use part of the lump sum of my pension to pay off the enormous debt I had incurred in trying to go into real estate. As a consequence of this I have less than a full pension to survive on, which is not adequate. Financially, life has been a struggle for me ever since.

For most of the next couple of years I found I actually enjoyed living by myself, enjoyed my own company. In all the years before this I had been miserable and lonely when I found myself living away from family or alone. Now was different. I felt I was finally my own person. I felt good about being independent.

The responses of both Hugo and Lenny to my coming out and the consequences of that were interesting but not unexpected. At the time I was a little surprised at Hugo; he was living in Melbourne and was an out gay young man so I think I expected more understanding from him. He was very angry at me for deserting Maeve in her condition and for not being honest with her for all those years. I feel a lot more relaxed with him now, and he with me, than we were.

I have tried to explain this here, so it remains to be seen how they both respond. There has been a lot of water under the bridge for both of them since I came out in 2000. Having graduated from Victorian College of the Arts, Hugo was a performer for many years and is now a highly qualified teacher with good prospects to advance. He lives with his husband, also a teacher, and is very settled.

Lenny was very angry and hostile towards me for many months after. I think, though he may not agree, that I did him a big favour in leaving him at home with Maeve when I left. At the time I left he was on a gap year and driving pizza delivery, drinking beer and smoking dope with his mates. I could see him easily slipping into this life with his mates in the Blue Mountains. My leaving seemed to force him to make some decisions on his own behalf. He left home at the end of that year and travelled to Europe to be with his girlfriend, Sue, who was studying in Germany. Upon his return he got a flat with a mate in Glebe and started university at Sydney Uni. He did very well, completed his master's degree and is now married to Sue with two beautiful children and a good career in local government.

Both my sons have done well, and I am so proud of them. I hope the years have taken the edge off their anger towards me. It is unfortunate that with Maeve now in care, the responsibility for her welfare has fallen to them.

Soon after leaving the house in Wentworth Falls, the Sydney Olympic Games was held. I went down to Sydney for a couple of days and the atmosphere in the city was really buzzy. Everyone was in a celebratory holiday mood, the games were broadcast on big screens all over the city, the trains all ran on time and 24/7. It was a good place to be.

Then I flew up to Townsville to stay a few days with Gary and Frank. I met Gary when I lived at the boys' hostel in the 1960's, we shared living arrangements when we were both flatting, and we stayed in touch over the years. He was a few years younger than me and came out as gay man sometime in his 20's. Gary met Frank at my wedding to Maeve and they had been together ever since. So, it was good to have a gay couple as friends and I enjoyed my time with them. They took me to a gay party; we went to a gay beach. It was good to be relaxed with them after all the years of me being hidden. I still see Gary occasionally. He and Frank are still together in Townsville, and I follow

Gary's adventures in Barcelona where he has another life.

It is such a relief, after all the years of struggle, of wanting life to be otherwise, to finally accept the truth of who I really am.

Chapter Forty-One

Falling in Love

I lived alone in the Blue Mountains around 2001. I was trying to work out where my finances were after the separation and signing the house over to Maeve. I was broke. All my money and the house went to Maeve. Meanwhile I was trying to gather enough to live on, pay my rent and try to save toward a deposit on a small house. I was not getting very far and felt completely weighed down and depressed by my dire financial situation.

About this time, I read an advertisement online about "how to make money in real estate without using your own money." I didn't have any money and was vulnerable to any offer where I might get enough to buy a house, so I signed up.

Sucked in.

I argued with myself that I had to spend money to make money. I was unhappy, alone, broke, unsure and vulnerable to talking myself into joining up. I was so gullible and uneducated in financial matters. I went to an introductory investment seminar in Brisbane, paid for with money I didn't have.

At the seminar, I met Ed, a handsome guy my age. The seminar was a rort, real rip-off — at least for people like me. I had enrolled and paid for a four-day weekend to learn about investing in real estate and getting rich. More expense. We met in this large auditorium on the first day. There would have been 2000 people in there. I didn't know anyone. We did some "team building" exercises and games and finished late, about 11 p.m. The next morning the speaker asked what people had done the previous evening. Most of us had headed to our rooms, reviewed the reading matter and headed for bed. This guy down from me announced that he'd gone dancing at a gay club in the Valley and had a great time. This seemed to be received with some disbelief, but I thought "How brave — foolhardy maybe — but it was brave to announce that in front of so many people."

After morning tea break, I walked back into the auditorium, thinking "I have four days to get through here, and I don't know a single soul. I need to make contact with someone." As I walked across the front of the tiered seats, I looked up the serried rows for a vacant seat. Halfway back there was a row of people with vacant seats at the end, and I saw this head of glowing grey hair in the first occupied seat; he was talking to the man next to him. His striking grey hair was luminous under the light, and I thought "That looks like a good place to start." I sat beside this man and eventually he stopped talking to the guy next to him and we greeted one another. I realised he was the same man who had announced his dancing night at the morning session. The guy next to Ed looked obviously gay and, as gays do, immediately I started talking to Ed he stopped and turned back to his own partner sitting next to him.

That's how I met Ed. I chose him from the crowd, drawn to him by fate. Ed was also married at this time, living with his wife and one adult child, the others having moved out. I had left home less than a year earlier, whereas Ed was still living at home, not "come out" as I had. I was attracted to Ed, tall, slim, grey hair, animated talker, charming, interesting and enthusiastic. Then he announced he was an architect, so to me this had to mean money: I was hooked. The universe was speaking to me!

That lunchtime I thought we could have a sandwich together, but he disappeared and didn't reappear until the afternoon session started. We talked occasionally that afternoon and he disappeared again at dinnertime then reappeared at the evening session. Again, we were in groups and did this rather alarming exercise where we put an arrow into our throat and then pressed on a board until the arrow broke — a "push and push through" exercise. Ed and I were in that group and shared the experience.

As the evening's sessions drew to a close, I suggested to Ed we go to his hotel and have a drink in the bar, which we did. Conversation began to flow as we relaxed, or at least I was relaxed. As I recall Ed gradually relaxed. I knew I was becoming increasingly enamoured with this handsome and intelligent man. He was ticking all the boxes for me. Tall, good looking, articulate, left leaning politically, married (so knew what I had come from), an architect — a professional and creative person, enthusiastic about the seminar we were at and the potential it was presenting to us. I knew I was falling for this guy, open to where it would lead — but where would that be? I knew I wanted it to be real, to continue, for me to belong.

As the conversation progressed Ed asked, "Well, are you gay?" and I replied, "Yes, I am. So, are you?" and he replied "Yes. But I'm still married." We were two adult men in the city alone, so inevitably I suggested then that we go up to his room and I would "Show you my etchings." But Ed declined, saying he was still married. Hmmm, seemed weird, "But I guess he's being careful" I rationalised. So, I returned to my hotel room alone. I didn't want to focus on the questions that came to the surface.

Both Ed and I had been married, had children, family life, careers and all the hetero expectations we both had thought we wanted at the time. Ed was still married to Fay. Yet at the time of my coming out a few months before meeting Ed, time for me wasn't real, it still wasn't what I really wanted or really was. With Ed I could see a future.

Though the marriage and kids bit was done with the best intentions, as the years progressed we had both come to realise that we were not being true to ourselves, our families or our partners. Life was like a mistaken dream. As much as we wanted it to be otherwise, the truth was different, scary and shameful. Yet we knew the truth had to be faced. Both of us in our own way had to make the decision to leave the marriage and face the consequences.

When we met it was, for me, like a bolt from the blue. I know now it was similar for many men when they first admit to themselves of their preference for men and fall in love with the first appealing man they come across.

Ed and I spent most of the remaining days sitting together and occasionally discussing the seminar, but other times Ed seemed to disappear without explanation. At one point toward the end we were asked to find others whom we could be partners with in working on investing in a property together. Ed and I linked up and I remember telling him that though I had a goodish income, after an expensive separation and property settlement I had no savings and no assets. He seemed confident that was no problem. I wanted to hear that and to see that he was confident, to believe that these hurdles could be overcome, as the speakers at the seminar assured us they could. I wanted to be assured we could make a go of it together, both as investment partners and as potential lovers. Ed assured me — and I wanted to be convinced — that we could help each other in achieving the first goal in any case.

At the end of the weekend, Ed returned to his matrimonial home and I returned to my rental house in the Blue Mountains. At occasional meetings we would discuss investment strategies and ways we could develop schemes that we could make work. We spent lots of money that I had to keep working on two jobs to earn, but there was little progress on either goal.

However, this man was still ticking all my boxes. He was sexy, loved dancing in gay clubs like I did, movies, theatre, partying. But no sex happened. One time I inveigled him to take a night away from home and we went to an hotel and made love for the first time. Neither of us had much experience. Ed had had a relationship with a man when he was a teenager and little since. But it was a very satisfying and sweet experience. I knew I had fallen in love with Ed, and making love with him was the first time I'd ever felt like a real man. All those years of marriage to Maeve, thinking this was it, that this was my lot, were blown away by this realisation. I finally felt whole.

During this early time, we would often go out dancing, taking party drugs, having a fantastic time together in each other's company. He was loving and attentive and considerate. We got on so well together. But at the end of the night, or by the early morning, Ed would simply announce he was "going home," and disappear from the dance floor. And I would be left at the end of the night, dancing alone, usually to go home man-less.

As a consequence, I had a series of boyfriends who were good for sex, and well, I thought maybe Ed would get the message. In retrospect, I should have woken up to him much earlier. But I didn't want to. Ed was the man for me. I loved him, and I stuck to him.

Chapter Forty-Two

Finding My Guru

It was about this time that I was going to a meditation group in Katoomba in the Blue Mountains and met an Australian "guru" who had spent a lot of time in India on his spiritual search. I found him a bit of a smooth talker/charmer but he suggested a trip to India to a group of us and, having minimally enough to cover the costs of this, I thought "Well, I'm free now so there is nothing stopping me."

I approached him and wanted to be included in the group. It was definitely worthwhile. India had been on my bucket list for years, but married life and Maeve's poor health meant it didn't happen.

Our guide gave us a very good overview of travel in India. He organised travel, accommodation, visits to holy sites and ashrams. He gave us an insight into spiritual travel in India that would have been far more difficult or impossible if he had not organised it for us. We trekked north of Rishikesh to the foot of the Himalaya, revisiting those amazing ranges and peaks I had fallen in love with twelve years before. We travelled down the Ganges by train and boat, and stopped at the main cities of Hardwar and Lucknow. We visited the Ghats of Varanasi, where I left the group and went exploring by myself. At one stage, I walked across the steps of the Ghats and gazed at the funeral pyres burning beside me as I passed. I tripped and slid down a couple of steps amongst the ashes of the pyres that were slippery with water and oils. Thank goodness I didn't break a hip or leg! It occurred to me that it would be a fine way to end it all on the Ghats of Varanasi. No one would know!

I met some interesting people and visited some interesting sites and ashrams but best of all was the introduction to the spiritual life of India. I had become aware some years earlier of an Indian holy man, Ramana Maharshi, who had lived in Tiruvannamalai in Tamil Nadu, the south of India. When I realised that Tiruvannamalai was included in the itinerary I was definitely interested. Ramana Maharshi, though he died three years after I was born, became my spiritual guru.

I travelled back to Tiruvannamalai three more times in the subsequent months. Though I stayed at the same ashram, each time was different, each time was a challenge in different ways. I enjoyed the people, the food was vegetarian, simple and tasty. The meditation around the ashram, in the temple meditation and the isolated meditation cave on the mountain were intense and inspiring experiences. Life in the ashram suited me at the time though there was always the pull of home and what that meant.

At the end of 2002, I returned to India for five weeks' holiday. This coincided with my move back to the inner city, but I would be home in time for that to happen. I was running away again; from the stress of trying to get back on my feet financially, the uncertainty of my relationship with Ed. Meditating and living in India was the escape I wanted.

A few days after I arrived in India, I received an email from Ed saying he had "left hearth and kin, was living south of the harbour, and missing his dancing partner." What to do? My holiday had just started but if he had said I want you to come back and be with me I would have. Then common sense got the better of me and I decided that no, that was his trip, India was mine, and I would join him when I got back to Oz.

India was again a great experience. I stayed at the Ramana Maharshi Ashram again in Tiruvannamalai. Ramana had lived there until 1950, establishing his reputation as a venerated holy man, and the ashram had been established in his honour. I slipped into the routine of meditation, lining up for the dining hall, sitting cross legged on the floor and eating vegetarian Indian food with my fingers; I loved the ceremony and the taste of the food. I would walk the mountain path up to the meditation cave that Ramana used, or farther down to another meditation cave that was pitch black inside. I sat for hours slowly breathing the spirit of the place. I really fell into the life of a follower of Ramana. Too soon the time came to an end and I had to return to Australia.

Taxi is probably the best of a bad lot if you want to get around India independently, economically and reliably. It is a five-hour trip by taxi from Tiruvannamalai to Chennai Airport. Five hours of stressful driving, traffic, unreliable roads, beaten up taxis and crazy taxi drivers, but it is still the best way to get around. So, I booked a cab to pick me up at the Ashram in Tiruvannamalai and drive me to the airport. I left about six hours to do it in and it was all paid for in advance. In retrospect I should have left at least seven hours.

The taxi arrived almost on time, a sigh of relief; being on time was a good start. I piled in with my luggage and we crawled through the local traffic of Tiruvannamalai to get to the main road, a usual two-lane tarmac. We had not gone far when the driver announced that he was picking up his "brother" to accompany us on the trip. Okay; what could I say? We collected this man and proceeded slowly through the traffic. After a while the taxi did not seem to be going as well as it should, and we limped along. Eventually he pulled over and insisted he look for a mechanic to "fix taxi." He did, and the taxi was quickly back on the road. Meanwhile the driver insisted I give him more money for the repairs. I gave him some of what I had left, not much, and said I would give him more when we got to the airport. I had no intention of doing anything like that. We proceeded through the traffic.

A fair while into the trip the taxi was again not performing very well, and we were going slower and slower along the road. Meanwhile the time was slipping away, and I could imagine that I would miss the plane. The driver insisted that he would need a "new taxi" so he drove into a town off the road. He edged his way into the centre of this town through traffic and markets and masses of people. Eventually he left me stranded in the taxi in a crowded street, while he and his "brother" went to look for another taxi. They seemed to be gone for ages. The time was ticking by rapidly with no progress to the airport. Here I was in a town I had no idea about, no idea where I was, no non-Indians to ask assistance from and no language to ask the locals.

Eventually he returned through the traffic with another taxi and insisted that I pay for the hire of the replacement. I told him I had already paid for the hire of the taxi to the airport but would give him more money when we got to the airport. He also had a new driver for the replacement taxi so, with me urging haste to make up time, we sped through the traffic, passing on the right-hand side and into the oncoming traffic, only getting over to the left when a huge truck loomed. Hair-raising to say the least.

We eventually arrived at the airport with only minutes to spare. I grabbed my bags from them and began running to the terminal. They were at me trying to get more money and I was trying to drag my bags and look like I was getting money for them as we ran. As I got closer to the terminal doors, I was relieved to see there was a security man there. I knew he would not admit the taxi guys following me, and I pushed through the doors. I ran to the check-in desk and made the last moment to check in for the flight, leaving the taxi guys to sort it out between themselves.

Tiruvannamalai was a very appealing retreat for me. It meant I was totally removed from any temptation to entertain my fantasies and remain removed from them. They were still present, but I found it easier to deal with them when I wasn't confronted by what I desired.

Chapter Forty-Three

Free and In Sydney

I had applied for a work transfer back to the Inner West and by the end of 2002 this was granted. I received a transfer from the public school in the western Sydney suburbs where I had been for the past seven years to a school in the Inner West of Sydney. As it happened, it was the first school I had worked at after graduating as a teacher in 1980.

So, at the beginning of 2003 after returning from India, I moved to Newtown and rented a little two-bedroom flat. It was mine, and I was happy living alone in Newtown again.

I started going to the Gay and Married Men's Association (GAMMA) meetings. It was a group for married men going through separation and trying to establish a new identity for themselves and cope with the trauma they were causing to the woman they had loved in their married life. It was an interesting group, and I met many men travelling through a similar journey to my own. After a year or two, I began to be the speaker at the fortnightly meetings on various topics. This was a good experience and gave something back to a group that had been so supportive of me. After Ed and I got together he came to the meetings as well, and I was proud of having my handsome partner to support me.

Around this time, I was at a gay social dance evening and saw a flyer advertising a "Men's Weekend" run by a group called Body Electric Oz. It warned that the weekend was "clothing optional" and designed to build self-confidence for men recently emerging as gay. Being single and up for new experiences, I said to myself "I can do that" and immediately enrolled. It was one of the best decisions I made in my development as a gay man.

Since that time my occasional involvement in Body Electric has enabled me to engage in self-development exercises and given me a greater sense of confidence in my mind, body, sexuality and relationships with gay men. It has exposed me to various activities and behaviours designed to increase my confidence and enjoyment of myself. In one exercise, we were in two circles facing each other. The facilitator would ask a question of the men in the inner circle or the outer circle. Questions such as: "What gifts has your father given you?" would send me into a spiral of emotion. The activities focussed on safety, giving, trust and touch such as holding and diorama. We would face each other and gaze into the partner's eyes without speaking. That can be a really intense exercise. Sometimes the partner would turn around and the other man would massage his back or shoulders.

Most activities are done naked, which allows participants to lose that self-consciousness associated with nakedness with other men. The activities themselves were in many cases variations of activities in alternate therapy; breath work, touch and massage, intense eye focus work that dispels the anxiety natural in men to that level of intimacy. What was always important was the sense of loving acceptance engendered by the organisers. At more advanced weekends the activities might be said to border on bondage and discipline (BDSM) but these activities, done in an atmosphere of love and trust, challenged the participants yet engendered a feeling of complete confidence and achievement. The results can be amazing when men feel safe and trusting in each other's company.

I was fortunate to participate as an "assistant" in many workshops, which gave me the opportunity to be more involved in the care and support of the men participating.

Participation in Body Electric workshops has brought me into contact with many men, beautiful in spirit and in heart, that have been a support and a pleasure to know. The experiences of Body Electric have increased my self-confidence as an adult gay man enormously.

Chapter Forty-Four

Ups and Downs with Ed

When I returned from India, Ed collected me at the airport and took me back to his flat. I stayed for three tortured nights of no sex and little communication. This was no good for me, so I left him to it and went back to my flat.

So, we were not having sex but still Ed wanted to go out dancing and partying with me. I wanted it too but tried to tell him that I also wanted to go home with him afterwards to make love. Such a simple thing did not happen. It was not to be.

I was still not noticing the warning signs. I saw Ed occasionally and was still in love with him. But really, two grown men, no family to consider and still no sex?! Come on!

One day at work I'd finally had enough. I wrote him a "vomit letter" — a four-page stream of consciousness diatribe. I drove to his flat and put the letter in his letter box. As I walked back to my car he drove up, not seeing me, but I saw him stop and pick up the mail from the letterbox. I walked up to him. He was surprised and pleased to see me, and we embraced – discreetly — in the daylight! He noticed the handwritten envelope from me and asked, "Did you write this?" So, we went down to the pontoon and he read the letter, tears and emotion ensued. We hugged on the pontoon and a ferry passing tooted its horn.

Was this a breakthrough? I had to leave as I had to get back to work, and left Ed to ponder his next move, or non-move. I was hoping for the best.

The next day we were to have a lunchtime meeting to discuss the latest financial disaster and our "strategies" to cope with it. We had coffee and talked a bit, but no mention of the letter or its contents. As I was walking back to my car, I remember thinking "Well, that's it." Nothing had been said. Then the phone rang. It was Ed inviting me to come to dinner that night at his place and to stay the night if I wanted to. I was overjoyed, nervously excited and wondering if it was real or not. I was glowing. Maybe what I wanted more than anything was about to happen.

So, we began a wonderful relationship that, in the early years, was exciting and fulfilling. There were still the difficult times when Ed was uncommunicative and moody. He obviously suffered from depression and anxiety. Was he on the autism spectrum? I wasn't sure. An adult with autism is not an easy person; does not have an easy life. He was a difficult man to live with at times. Never angry or threatening to me but nevertheless there were many times I did not feel I could communicate with him on any level.

With all the doubts, Ed prevailed. I was really in love with him, though early on I had doubts about his practicality and his seemingly unrealistic approach to money, debt and many other things. Even then the alarm bells were going off, but I was in love with him. He was an architect, which meant a lot to me because he had the potential to earn good money. I hoped all would settle down after a while. It never did.

He used to drive me crazy with his attitude to money, his increasing inability to complete work to the stage where he could get paid for it and have some money coming in, his need to borrow money to survive all the time, his mucking around and "stir crazy" behaviour with the dogs, staying up all night supposedly working, and then rushing to finish a job and having to deliver it on the knocker. Sometimes he produced really good work and received the accolades from clients that he deserved, but a lot of the time it was like getting blood out of a stone to get his contracts to that point.

So, we got into debt, and I followed his advice because I loved him and wanted to be with him; that's what you do when you're with someone you love — it's the way life is. I thought that because he was the architect, he would know what he was doing. I was hoping that it would all work out for the best and we would make some money to get us going. Besides, I didn't know what else to do.

Chapter Forty-Five

Dealing with Looming Disaster

In the early weeks and months of our relationship, beginning from when Ed and Fay were still living together, the three of us began a financial business arrangement. This was at the urging of Ed but with my encouragement and co-operation and his wife's agreement. The agreement was to use our combined incomes and equity in their family home to invest in real estate with the prospect of "increasing wealth." My specific goal, which I made clear to them, was to make enough money to invest in my own house and be paying it off by the time I reached sixty years of age.

At this time early in our relationship Fay was unaware that Ed and I were lovers. It must have been a bombshell for her when she found out.

Ed, Fay and I had a busy and interesting time, which gradually went pear-shaped as we realised that we had let ourselves be duped into buying off the plan and investing in developments that were not as profitable as the developers and prospectuses indicated. With a combination of naivety and desperate enthusiasm to succeed, we found ourselves in a financial hole that became increasingly complicated, expensive and desperate.

Ed talked us into purchasing two townhouses in a group of four in Newtown. I was uncertain and said I would be happy trying for one, but Ed insisted we pay a deposit on two of the houses, so Fay and I fell in behind him. It wasn't long before settlement was due, and we could not raise the finance for both. So, we had to forfeit the deposit on one of the townhouses; a huge loss that Ed argued we would cover on the increase in value of the house. Nevertheless, it was debt we had to cover before we could start to make a profit.

A similar scenario occurred later with an apartment off the plan in Melbourne. Ed was a professional, he should know! So, we agreed and went into a purchase with the three of us. At Ed's urging we again went into a debt we could not finance. In the end we had to dispose of the apartment at over $100,000 less than we had agreed to pay for it. Another huge loss. We, and importantly I, were losing money at a rapid rate and getting further into debt.

Additionally, the solicitor we had earlier engaged to handle the purchase of the Melbourne unit, a friend of Ed's, cost us dearly. He mismanaged the allocation of the title shares on the Newtown property we bought (or the bank owned) and didn't pay our mortgage on the due date, thus defaulting on the mortgage and again costing us dearly financially and mentally.

After Ed moved out of the family home into his own rented flat, Fay began divorce proceedings against him. This became increasingly angry and unpleasant and I, as a partner in the financial arrangements and investments, became caught up in this most unpleasant web. This was exacerbated by the solicitors engaged by Fay who appeared to constantly change the settlement demands on Ed and myself without acknowledging what had already been agreed. The daily stress Ed and I were experiencing was horrendous.

I felt enormously for Ed because of Fay's unrelenting anger, the changing demands, the lack of funds and his general mental health. I was also in extreme stress, anxiety and worry. I was trying as much as possible to stay positive, to support Ed, to continue working at my full-time job and my evening counselling work to make money to pay the mortgage expenses, solicitors bills, and try to meet the financial responsibilities I had got myself into.

I had a lingering sympathy for Fay and understood her anger. She had got herself into debt by agreeing with Ed and going into our "investments," but she was also aware she had lost her partner and I, the third party in this arrangement, was the one who was now his lover. She was depressed, overweight and unhappy, but I think she also had a major part in their separation.

I began to see that not only did I have no chance of achieving my retirement goals, I was getting deeper and deeper into a morass of debt that I didn't have any way of extricating myself from without huge loss. It was an emotionally draining, mentally exhausting and very depressing time.

Ed and I managed to raise a mortgage to buy a dilapidated but large terrace in Newtown. It was a house with good bones that needed so much work to bring it up to an acceptable standard. But it was basically a good house and a good investment in an up-and-coming inner-city suburb. I loved that house and could see that it would be a good way for Ed and I to lift ourselves out of our financial mess. Again, with Ed's urging he and I took an "interest only" loan, which meant the payments were more affordable, but the capital of the loan did not get reduced month by month. We did some much-needed work on the house much of which I was able to finance from my savings and working. There was a lot of work to be done and the house swallowed money like water.

I was still broke and working hard, long hours trying to make headway financially. I constantly had to loan money to tide Ed over for his mortgage share, household bills, food and holidays. At the same time, I felt so much compassion for him having to deal with his ex and his family. Their behaviour toward him made me despair for him. Ed was a good man with a generous and loving heart, he loved his children and grandchildren, and he tried to make amends with his ex, but at every turn he was rejected, criticised, marginalised and wounded. I have seen him heartbroken at their lack of support and the disrespect they have loaded on him, except for his daughter Maz who remained loyal to him. He needed my support and I tried to give it. I did my best for Ed during this time and continued to do so for some time.

He was dependent on me for emotional and financial support. I knew his life was difficult and I felt for him intensely. His life was full of stress and anxiety caused by family discord and financial matters, involving expensive lawyers and recalcitrant litigators, but this somehow brought us closer together, stronger and more determined to get through whatever was thrown at us. My love and compassion for Ed was sorely tested during those times. I was with him and supported him as he went through the punishment he endured from his ex-wife and the family and the lawyers. It was heart wrenching. I felt so much compassion and concern for him.

One night I arrived home from my night job and Ed was not there. It was not unusual for him to be away at a meeting, but he was usually home mid-evening for a late meal. As the evening wore on, I wondered about his well-being. He had experienced months of mental and emotional stress that was unrelenting and so difficult. I was concerned for his mental well-being and worried about him. His brother had committed suicide in his thirties, and he told me he had contemplated suicide in the past.

I had been ringing his phone and by late evening, I was concerned enough to ring his phone several times, but he didn't respond. I rang a few friends he might have visited for a drink, worrying them at a late hour, to check if they knew of his whereabouts but they hadn't seen him. About 1 a.m. he rang in response to my desperate voicemails. My blood froze when I asked him where he was and he replied, "The Gap" — a popular Sydney suicide spot.

What to do?

I talked to him for some time and offered to bring him home but he refused, saying he was OK and would drive himself home. I waited anxiously another thirty minutes and he arrived. I was much relieved but realised this was a good indication of his current state. I felt so sad and concerned for him. I was also angry that I had allowed myself to get into this mess. Ed was so rash in his decisions and his ex-wife was so difficult and determined in her dealings with us over these financial matters. I also felt some shame for her because of my role in this mess. But hey, this is the way life is, however unpleasant. Fay had a lot to deal with but she proved she was not an adaptable person and was urged on by her relentless solicitor. It had got to a breaking point for both of us.

Chapter Forty-Six

Fun Times with a Good Man

In addition to the difficult times Ed and I had, we had lots of fun times to relax and let off the pressure we were under. We still had fun and really enjoyed each other's company. We loved dancing shirtless at hot dance parties, taking party drugs in moderation at parties, staying up all night at the big dance parties, dancing with each other in the company of friends.

Phoenix, a dance club in a cellar on Oxford Street, was a favourite. They played fantastic music through a great sound system, and there were lots of shirtless, sweaty men dancing and enjoying each other. I loved being the first on the dance floor with Ed, moving erotically to the music. I'd "warm up" and take my shirt off, showing off my dance moves to the crowd — "Watching me watching you."

One hot summer night after midnight we were high and drunk and driving home in Ed's little Fiat Box. We had our shirts off and were enjoying the breeze as we sped up Cleveland Street. Turning the corner into City Road our hearts sank as we were waved into a police breathalyser check-point. Ed slowed down and followed the police signals. We were waved along the row of police checkers toward the front of the line. As it happened the last car of the previous lot was just leaving the line-up, so Ed just kept following him and drove out the other end. Meanwhile, the cops just watched us drive by as we kept driving. All the way home we were yelling our heads off about the cops chasing us. We switched the lights off and parked the car and bolted into the house nervously laughing our heads off! A lucky escape.

Playbox was another great party that was held in a "big top" at Luna Park. They also played fabulous music through a wonderful sound system. I loved the lasers and seas of shirtless, sweaty men that greeted us upon arrival. On the party drugs and a couple of drinks I was in seventh heaven. Such abandoned bliss.

Other favourites were the Mardi Gras parties held after the Pride Parade and a party called "Sleaze." Sleaze was a fabulous gathering held at the showground about two or three times a year that Ed and I always found the money to attend. It was really fun.

The first time we were together at Sleaze, we danced in the Royal Hall of Industries (RHI), an extensive pavilion in the middle of a huge seething mass of shirtless, sweaty men. Having taken a party drug, we were dancing facing each other under a spotlight, moving to the music and enjoying each other. He was so handsome and me so in love with him at that moment. Suddenly Ed leaned into me and said, "I have to go." I knew this was him just running away from a challenging situation.

"No," I said. "Stay with me, Ed. Just look into my eyes and stay with me."

He did. We danced looking into each other's eyes, holding hands, dancing quietly with each other and he, much to his credit, stayed calm, safe and secure with me through that time. I felt great.

Those were wonderful days, wonderful parties. The time was all too short, as it was brought crashing to a close by government legislation that suppressed the parties despite the generally sensible, mature behaviour of the participants. The drug dogs and the police were so threatening and oppressive.

Dance tickets were really expensive, so we made a point of buying them when they first came on sale as they were cheapest then. Arriving by taxi in a pouring storm at one "Sleaze Party," Ed and I made a dash from the taxi to the entrance. Before we left home, we each had carefully taped two Es in our underpants. A phalanx of police and drug dogs waited in the rain to pounce. Surely in the rain any smell from the Es would be disguised? No, unfortunately. One immediately pointed out Ed. I heard this loud anguished cry of my name and thought "Damn I hope Ed can get through this." Ed told me later that when he was challenged about having drugs, he admitted to having two Es on him. He was taken to be searched and pointed them out to the police. I saw Ed taken to be searched as I stood under some shelter from the rain. Soon after, a drug dog sat next to me and a policewoman said, "The dog has pointed you out. Do you have drugs on you?'"

"No," I replied.

"Then how do you explain the drug dog pointing you out?"

"Well," I replied, "we shared a joint just before we left home less than thirty minutes ago and maybe it can smell the smoke on me."

She looked at me disparagingly and said, "You'll have to be searched."

"Fine," I said, thinking what if they find the pills in my jocks?

I was taken to another enclosure to be searched. The policeman then went through my clothes and felt my legs, looked in my boots, turned my leather jacket inside out and so on. Though he felt up my legs into my crotch where the Es were, he didn't go high enough. I was allowed to enter the party.

But where was Ed? I waited for him inside and eventually he arrived. I felt for him. They had found the pills in his underwear and taken his dance ticket and not returned it. "The dance promoters don't want your type attending the party," they had told him. Poor guy, even though he didn't have much money, he had to buy another ticket at full price to get into the party. He had his drugs confiscated, so I gave him one of mine, which meant I only had one too!

I was really offended by this treatment. Here we were more than mature age adults, playing in moderation, only wanting to maximise our enjoyment while remaining in control. The police had no recognition of our maturity and experience. Sure, many others who do party drugs are not mature, but we were. The State was treating us as common gutter criminals. And the fun police — the religious right, the conservatives and the anti-gay lobby — were ruining our right to enjoy ourselves. Did we try to upset their right to political and religious freedom? Not a bit. But they did their darndest to ruin ours, and unfortunately their psychological and economic warfare succeeded. It became unviable for promoters to continue to host dance clubs and parties and our world is the poorer for it.

At a meeting held by the Inner-City Legal Service (ICLS) to discuss police drug dog action, I volunteered to help man an information service at the next party. The ICLS had a booth inside the gates to support any patron found with drugs in their possession. Meanwhile, volunteers like me were rostered to roam outside and support any patron pointed out by the drug dogs and taken off for questioning and body searching by the police. I had a 12 to 2 a.m. slot so it was a pretty dark and forbidding place with the dogs and police around outside the entrance. I was required to address any partygoer who left the search vans to go to the party. At one stage I asked a female partygoer who was being escorted back from the search vans to the party by a policeman as I was supposed to do: "Are you okay?"

The police officer immediately turned on me and an inch from my face screamed, "Of course she's okay. We are here to keep you safe!"

I froze but responded quietly, "Fine." It's that self-talk again — telling myself to stay calm.

That verbal violence sent me into a momentary traumatic decline, and I was shaking with nerves for a while, but proud that I was able to stand my ground. I have never felt so unsafe as when police are insisting that they are here to keep us "safe." It is such an abuse of power. And I don't think that cop believed what he was saying.

Around this time Ed and I were having coffee with a friend, Carl, and he happened to mention that he had found return tickets to Tokyo for less than $1000 if anyone was interested in coming with him. I had the money available and jumped at the chance. Japan has never been high on my bucket list, mainly because of the role they played in World War 2 and the effect on my father and on me. But this fare was too good to pass up.

A few months later Carl and I flew to Tokyo. From the moment we landed I was amazed and in love with Japan. The size of the buildings, the huge cities and CBD's, the huge hotels and the enormous number of people. We spent two days in Tokyo then caught the bullet train, another eye-opener because of its speed and punctuality, to Nagasaki. The site of the atom bomb impact was a dignified and impressive memorial to Japan's loss. After two days in Nagasaki we took the train to Kyoto, a wonderful older city. We took a final day back in Tokyo before flying home.

I was impressed by many things about Japan, not least the size of the cities and buildings, the sheer volume of people, the punctuality of trains, the simple beauty of the gardens. It was all so ordered and clean and relaxed. I'm glad I went.

So back home to Ed and dealing with the difficulties of finances and life in general.

Chapter Forty-Seven

Cambodia and Vietnam

For a while I'd been contemplating volunteer work in an overseas country helping on a worthwhile project to better the lives of the people there. I came across a group called Habitat for Humanity that had a program for volunteers that involved building homes for the inhabitants that they could not afford themselves. For years I had known about the devastation of the Pol Pot years on Cambodia, and from what I'd read the Cambodians were beautiful, gentle people who had fallen under the power of this brutal despot. The regime had wreaked havoc on the people, their lifestyle and on the country itself.

Cambodia had been a peaceful and apparently safe and prosperous country before the Vietnam War, and then Nixon had decided to bomb the very existence of Cambodia off the planet because it was considered a training ground for the Viet Cong. Apparently, more bombs were dropped on Cambodia, a small and underdeveloped country, than on all the cities of Europe in the Second World War. One can only imagine the devastation and disruption that caused the Cambodian people. Out of that devastation emerged Pol Pot and his regime of oppression, torture, displacement and further devastation.

Habitat for Humanity built homes for the people of Phnom Penh. This seemed a worthwhile project to get involved with, so I signed up to be included in a work party to go to there. It wasn't all that much money, and as a volunteer I was expected to work on constructing a house for the people. I reasoned that would be fine as I had lots of experience in renovations and building.

Vietnam was just next door, so I wanted to include it in my itinerary. I tried to talk Ed into meeting me in Vietnam and having a holiday, but he was very reticent, mostly because of the cost. So, I agreed to shout him the airfare, and he agreed to meet me in Saigon after my two weeks in Cambodia.

I have difficulty talking about my response to Cambodia. It was incredibly depressing, and I was so affected by what had been visited on the people by Pol Pot and his regime. The disruption of their lives, the senseless torture and mass murder. There was a "museum" of photographs of the people who were tortured and murdered; men, women and children. Hundreds and hundreds of poor quality black and white snaps formed a very poignant illustration of the senselessness of this mass execution. Similarly, in the Museums of the Oppression there were the instruments of torture showing how these poor, innocent people were heartlessly tortured, degraded and murdered. And the poverty. I was stunned by the extreme desperation of the people evident in the streets, villages and markets. In India even the extremely poor people had an energy about them, but I found the people of Cambodia seemed to have no spirit in them, like it had been torn out.

My response was almost a type of inactivity, a loss of my own ability to be active and positive, a helpless response to the hopelessness of their situation. I felt devastated for them and ashamed at my own lack of response. I enjoyed building the brickwork of the houses we were working on, though it only seemed like we were building the slums of the future because they were sited side by side, with floor size the space of a car garage, no area around them and no facilities to be had in the vicinity. Additionally, there appeared to be a lot of corruption in their lives, a lot of "strong men" with money driving black SUVs with tinted windows that blasted their foghorns at them if they were in the way. This corruption appeared to have such a negative effect on their lives.

We visited poor families who lived in shanties built on poles above foetid water. We visited the "floating villages" where people seemed without hope or energy. There were no facilities, no money, no work. There were countless unfortunate souls who had lost limbs to landmines. We saw where babies had been bashed to death on trees, where people had been tortured and maimed in horrific and inhuman ways in prison and camps. This was one of the hardest things to deal with. I have been amazed at my poor response to this experience. How I have left these people to their plight and not attempted to assist them beyond what I did then leaves me feeling useless, ineffectual and selfish.

This trauma, carried from my early years with Dad, the bullying by Warwick Patterson and Victor Jarvic, various people's aggressiveness to me in the work environment, the threatened attacks from the driver in North Thailand, always engendered the same response. I was immobilised, unable to act for my own benefit or that of others.

Trauma and bullying have an ongoing impact all through life, as they have in mine. It is only in later years that I have been able to deal with this in a positive way, standing up to people that have tried to bully me. The experience in Cambodia was especially affecting because I was immobilised by the trauma of others, powerless to assist and to get myself to a position where I have felt able to be involved positively with them.

I enjoyed living in Phnom Penh for about two weeks as a "foreigner," staying in a hotel and exploring the city. I'd go out for a run in the early morning, steaming and sweating like the local city dwellers in the humidity of the city, back to the hotel for breakfast before we assembled for the bus trip to our worksite.

After that it was time to travel to Vietnam and Saigon and meet up with Ed. We had a good holiday travelling from Saigon to Ho Chi Min City up the coast and then to Howlong Bay and the highlands. I loved Vietnam as a comparison to Cambodia. Vietnam had energy, the people were friendly and independent, the hotels were fine, the traffic was stupendous, the food was really good. The hills of rock and the trees rising out of Howlong Bay were quite spectacular.

I tried out the way we were told to cross the street: find a gap and start walking and keep going, don't stop whatever you do and you'll get to the other side. And it worked. It took a bit of holding the breath and hoping for the best but once the traffic knew you were intent on crossing, they all seemed to just go around you.

Ed seemed a bit distant and depressed. I was paying for his major expenses and he may have felt that a bit. But I was taking that as it may and accepting that I was supporting him in the hope his depression might ease, and that he might become more energetic with work. But really this was a lost cause.

Chapter Forty-Eight

Chrysstina

For many years after she was adopted out as a baby, we could not do anything about finding Chrysstina's whereabouts. The government website, and before that the department enquiries line, would not consider any approach by any person other than a direct birth relative. Fair enough.

Bill, Alice, myself and occasionally other members of the family would speak about this vacant part in our family and how it would be so good to find a connection to the person we had lost. We also discussed how difficult it was for us that Maree was determined to not allow any contact with her child. We approached her intermittently but, to our knowledge, she remained unflinchingly adamant that she would not countenance any attempt to contact Chrysstina.

I felt really torn by this, as I wanted to understand and accept Maree's decision, yet I also knew the anguish of others who were denied for whatever reason in finding their birth family. During my many years of teaching and counselling, I had talked with or worked with clients or colleagues, people who had been adopted by loving parents and been given all the love and support a child should receive. Yet there was still a hole in their lives. It wasn't always evident, but not knowing their birth parent or family history made their lives more difficult. Most did not want to offend or trouble their adoptive family and refused to seek out their blood relatives or were stopped from doing so by the reaction of their parents. However, this unresolved matter sat heavily in their lives.

I felt this may well be how Chrysstina felt. I could have been gravely mistaken, but that is how my heart felt. We had held this lost child in our hearts for decades. We had a connection to her before she was born. The whole family, with the exception of Maree, felt the same.

Maree and Ian, her husband, chose to live a childless life. Ian was involved in work and restoring cars, while Maree worked and was an elder in her church. As years went by, we found out she had approached Ian about locating Chrysstina but he had "thrown a hissy" and refused. Apparently, he said, "You wouldn't have any of my children, so I am not having another man's children in my home." Not a surprising response but nevertheless very difficult for Maree.

We discussed the fact that Maree could make a decision on this for herself, but by this time she had been caught up in a demanding fundamentalist church whose strict tenets dictated a wife should be subject to and obey her husband. Maree had swallowed this hook, line and sinker, and would not disobey her husband or tarnish her reputation in the church.

How could she deny — punish, really — her own child by not acknowledging her? How could she submit to her husband when it appeared to go against the natural order of things? Hence, we had to grudgingly accept Maree's decision because the state declared we were powerless to intervene. Although time and state attitudes have changed, Maree never has.

Many years passed, and Alice discovered the stipulations on who could apply to locate adopted family members had changed. When she called, a person in a registry told her there was no person of that name seeking contact or information. Decades passed before Alice alerted me to a website that provided a message board for those seeking contact with an adopted relative. This was a complete long shot as it would depend on the person at the other end searching and finding the relevant message. However, I left a message on the website with the details I had. It turns out I had the wrong birthday by a few days and the wrong birth hospital! Silly me! Anyway, I put this brief message on the message board with a final few words saying "We are a large family of uncles and aunts who hold you in our hearts and would dearly love to welcome you into our family." I clicked "post" and thought nothing more of it.

A good eight or ten months later, my mobile rang. I was busy at work, and I generally do not answer numbers when the name does not register in my contacts. Something made me answer this call, though.

"Hello?"

"Are you Tony Williams?" a woman said.

"Well, here's the start of a sales pitch. I wonder what she's selling..." I thought. I said curtly, "Yes. How can I help you?"

"Did you put an ad....?" she was speaking quietly, and I couldn't hear her.

"What are you talking about?" I asked impatiently, not making it easy for her. Thank goodness she persevered.

"Well, I am responding to a message left in this 'Find an Adoptee' website."

I froze!

"Right," I responded, "What's your name?"

"Chrysstina," she said.

Oh my god, I went into shock. For a moment I couldn't think, I couldn't get my breath, my heart was in my mouth, I couldn't get a word out. My mind was racing. Maybe this is Chrysstina. Maybe she has found us! We spoke for a few minutes, and I figured she was who she said she was. We agreed to meet, but ever unsure I asked, "How will I know you?"

Being a modern girl, she responded "I'll send you a selfie!"

Of course! It never occurred to me! A few moments later I had the spitting image of Maree on my phone. I was astounded. I could not believe the image I was looking at. Blonde hair, blue eyes, same jawline, same skin, attractive, beautiful teeth and smile. It was definitely the Chrysstina that we had been searching for all these years. Forty-four years had passed, and we were to be reunited!

I sent her a selfie of me and boy I looked forty-four years older. Not that she would notice! She was over the moon. As she related, finally she had found herself, where her looks came from, her mannerisms, her intelligence, her sunny disposition, why she looked so different to everyone else in her family. As things progressed, she needed that sunny disposition, it would be sorely tested again and again.

We would have travelled across the state for her, but agreed to meet at Manly Wharf, north of the Sydney Harbour. On the appointed day I met Bill, Alice, Donny and Jack at Circular Quay and we headed over to Manly on the Manly Ferry and to the wharf. We were sitting, chatting and waiting and there was a blonde woman looking the other way nearby, so I went over and asked, "Are you Chrysstina?" She was! She was so happy to meet us. We were stunned by how familiar she looked; the image of our sister Maree was beaming at us. She exclaimed at how similar we looked to her. It's true, the family resemblances were unmistakeable. Her first question to us was "Do I have any siblings?" Obviously, a sense of where she fitted into this family was of paramount importance.

There were so many similarities between our family and Chrysstina even though we'd had no contact since birth. Chrysstina had just completed a degree at Macquarie Uni, a late starter academically as we were. She had a disrupted schooling (like many of her uncles and aunts!), suspended when she was fifteen for smoking dope, living with her partner at sixteen (all so familiar!). They are still together. Chrysstina is blessed with a bright and warm nature, loving her children and partner, caring for others in her professional career.

Life had not been easy for her. Her adoptive father died when she was still quite young, and her mother moved overseas leaving her to manage her own life in Australia. From this difficult beginning Chrysstina has emerged a beautiful, warm, intelligent and resilient woman, and a real attribute to humanity. Behaviours and attributes attest to the power of nature in this genetic inheritance! It was absolutely wonderful to be able to welcome her into our family, apart from the one big sadness we still had to deal with, and support Chrysstina in dealing with as best we could. The happiness and relief were overlaid by this sadness about her mother's continued denial and rejection.

Maree heard what had transpired and, as I had been the contact point, my name was yet again mud! Maree despised me and she furiously vented her anger at me for having the gall to go against what she had forbidden. I had no contact with Maree over this: it is only what has been relayed to me by others of the family, in-laws and nieces. Alice was also at the receiving end of Maree's ire, and Alice and Bill along with the other brothers have little if anything to do with Maree.

It is true that we had gone completely against Maree's wishes in this, however we felt giving Chrysstina the opportunity to meet her birth relatives and family was the right thing to do. Though I have no regrets about finding

Chrysstina and welcoming her into her own family, I am sad and sorry that her own mother continues to reject her. I have apologised to Chrysstina for possibly making her life harder, but she is happy that we did. She has had the opportunity of meeting us and of knowing from where she comes.

Chrysstina and her husband and children have been welcomed to a number of family Christmases and functions, but each of which Maree has insisted she be informed so that she will not attend and will not meet face to face with her.

Sometime later another surprise emerged. Alice has contacts over the years with people who are involved in the music industry. She was conversing with an old muso friend one night who happened to mention that he played a few gigs in a band called Chrysstina in the early 70's. This immediately sparked Alice's interest! When questioned if he had known a member of the band called Jason Blunt, he didn't recall but gave her the name of another muso who had had a longer involvement with the group.

Alice jumped at the chance and sent this guy an email. He responded with the information that Jason had not been shot, was indeed alive and well, though he didn't have a contact for him. He reported that Jason was still working in the music industry and in fact lived on the northern beaches, not far from Chrysstina and her family. Some months later Alice received an email from Jason saying he was very much alive. Alice contacted Jason and discussed Chrysstina with him. As you would imagine he was very surprised as he had assumed, after what Mackie had said to him all those years ago, that the baby was non-existent, that the pregnancy had been terminated. Alice informed him otherwise. Our short experience of Jason at the time of Maree's pregnancy indicated that he was a lively, friendly but probably flighty muso. He was very interested in the news but wanted to talk it over with his wife and adult daughter. This would have been a challenge for him as well, coming completely out of the blue after all these years.

Apparently, his wife hit the roof and declared that she would leave if he had anything to do with Chrysstina, that she was not prepared to open her home to a child of his past.

It was tragic for Chrysstina — rejected by both parents. Neither of them gave her the benefit of the doubt or the honour of at least acknowledging her and explaining their stance. Both allowed their partners to dictate their decision and rejected Chrysstina out of hand. Their own child. So difficult, so sad.

A postscript to this story is that recently Jason and Chrysstina have been in touch. That's all I know. Small steps but it's good news.

Chapter Forty-Nine

Ed Loved the Dogs

I had forked out tens of thousands of dollars to mainly fund essential structural renovation that needed to be done on our "new" house before we would be able to move on to renovations on the interior. We replaced the roof of the upstairs rear rooms, excavated under the floor, demolished the lower floor structure and replaced it with new flooring and joists, and installed a 2000 litre tank under the floor for future use. We installed new plumbing and waste pipes under the house. These were all major, costly and essential to do before we could begin work on the new upstairs bathroom and other renovations.

The other issue that was bubbling along concerned dogs. We had taken care of Hugo's two dogs, Claude and Ivy, when he moved back from Melbourne. Ed loved the dogs and they would keep him company as he worked or roistered with them in his workroom upstairs. Eventually Claude died of old age, leaving tiny one-eyed Ivy, a stunted miniature chihuahua. Ed insisted we get a second dog. Hence Susie, a beautifully natured foxie bitzer "rescue" dog, became part of the family. I was happy for Ed to have a second dog, a quiet one, to keep him company as I believed it would be good for him and his depression while he spent long hours at his work. Ivy wasn't too keen but she tolerated Susie.

Not long after that Ed began to agitate for a third dog. I was not happy about that because of the mess they made of the house and the costs of the food bill. Ed also loved to play rowdily, having them running around the house, sliding on the mats, chasing upstairs and downstairs, throwing balls in the house and generally completely razzing them. I was trying to maintain an ordered house because we were continually renovating. I ran a business that had clients coming to our home, and I expected a reasonably clean house to do it in.

Ed had some friends who occasionally went on holiday and, soft hearted as he is, he agreed to look after their dog, as we had a couple of times. It was a stupid fluffy animal with long floppy ears that used to dangle in the water bowl when he was drinking and then he would flip-flop around the house spraying water everywhere. Not only did I not want another dog in the house, I didn't want to have to mind a dog for someone who was just avoiding paying kennel fees. Again, I was frustrated and furious. Ed knew I didn't want a messy dog in the house, but he was caught between me and refusing these "friends." My argument was that they were simply using him, and me, as a cheap way of getting their dog minded. Anyway, one morning I was in bed and suddenly this dog appeared flopping all over the place and landed on the bed! I was so angry I stood up in bed and roared. That took him back a step. I can't remember what happened but that was the last time we had that dog, and so much for those friends. I don't think Ed has seen them since either.

Chapter Fifty

Bawley Point – Gannet Beach

A way for me to have a respite from this continual stress was to escape down the south coast of NSW to my friend Bron's house. Bron is an older single woman I met when we lived in Wentworth Falls. We had kept contact over the years. She was supportive of me over all that time of Maeve's illness and incapacity. Bron is an inspiration to me. She is a very independent and resourceful woman. She worked for a couple of months in East Timor and has earned her doctorate. She has been an independent spirit all her life. After leaving the Blue Mountains she moved to the inner city for a few years and then finally down the coast at Bawley Point. I absolutely loved the spot she chose. Unfortunately, Bawley Point is one of the small towns that was devastated in the recent bushfires.

Bron's house was a short, level walk from Gannet Beach, a perfect curve of white sand. The water was so clear and crisp, the waves regular and easy. I would get up early and be the only one at the beach for a swim in the beautiful clear mornings. The water was superb and the swimming beautiful. I could swim up and down the beach in delicious cool clean water. Alone.

On the South Coast it is generally cooler; mild summers, beautiful, sunny warm days. Not hot in spring, leading into summer. By the end of January though the days start to get noticeably less hot, the sun less fierce. Summer is moving into a mild autumn. By the end of January when the holidaying families have departed, the heat has gone, there is just the mild fine days, still warm enough to swim, but not so hot that you sweat and can't stand the heat.

These are the days I loved being at Gannet Beach. The mild days, the air now a little chilly in the early morning as I walked down from the house to the beach for my morning swim. I loved being totally alone, the beach deserted. The water was so clear, transparent aqua, clean, the smell of salt, the regular soft waves gently collapsing on the clear white sand of the perfect curve of the beach. It felt sublime as I dropped my towel, my shirt and cap, and walked languidly to the water's edge, feeling the bubbling caress of the end of each wave as it reached my toes, ankles, thighs, body.

Then the dive into the mild clear water to start my swim.

Gannet is such an easy beach to swim most days, the water is sweet and clear, the right coolness, the clarity matching the sky above. Fresh, clear, clean, unspoiled. I feel so alone, there is no one there, just the water, the day, and me, slowly swimming the curve of the beach and back again.

One morning swimming out from the beach I felt this hard brush against my leg. I looked down to see a manta ray swimming past me, its large wings slowly propelling it along. I gradually regained my breath and resumed my swim.

Then I could sit at the house and read all day. In the afternoon we would go for a walk up the next beach, Murramarang, a beautiful beach named in the local dialect. I loved the spot. I was sad when she sold it and moved back to the Blue Mountains to be near her adopted family. Now she lives near my son and the grandchildren. It means a lot to me to see Bron and have a good catch-up.

Chapter Fifty-One

Bobbie Blue

Though Ed might not have the money to meet his financial obligations, he had the money to get another dog! Ed's agitation finally wore me down and I agreed to a third dog. So, I relented, against my better judgement and common sense, thinking this might satisfy him. Thus began the short but eventful saga with Bobbie Blue — another beautiful foxie bitzer dog. This one was the alpha male, with a beautiful nature but very active, lively and gregarious. He needed lots of exercise and attention. Charming, attractive, charismatic — yes, a dog can be charismatic! Bobbie Blue was charismatic in spades. He was well loved by the staff at the doggy rescue place, and had been cared for by a couple who fostered dogs from the centre; he was a favourite. They doted on Bobbie Blue.

Ed had seen Bobbie Blue on the website and insisted on being allowed to take him as an adoption. Bobbie Blue lasted about six months. One morning a day or two before Christmas we woke to find Bobbie in dreadful spasm. It seemed pretty obvious that he was suffering from a tick bite. We were puzzled though as he had not been out of the Inner West and we didn't believe there were ticks in the inner city. However, he was certainly very ill and needed urgent treatment.

Ed immediately took him to the local vet where you would reasonably expect effective support. He was referred to the small animals' hospital as the local vet couldn't treat him. The next thing I know I got a call from Ed at the hospital saying that he needed to pay $2000 up front before they would treat Bobbie. Ed was distraught. As per usual he did not have any funds. I had no choice but to deal with the staff member there and agree to pay $2000 on my credit card. This was just before Christmas!

They kept Bobbie overnight. They called Ed during the night to say things were not getting worse or better, and they had not found the reason why the dog was so ill. Eventually they rang with the news that Bobbie had died. Ed was beside himself and drove out to get Bobbie's body. However, I then received a call from Ed, crying, that they wanted the account settled before they would release the body.

I was furious and felt trapped. I was tempted to refuse to pay but I couldn't because Ed was in such anguish. The balance was another $2650 for a total of $4650 on my credit card. And only two days before the expenses of Christmas. I was furious and frustrated. All that money wasted, they were the "specialists" and they let the damn dog die anyway!

I was so indignant at their treatment and angry at the gouging they had done on us. It seemed such an exorbitant amount to pay. Eventually I composed a letter to the veterinary hospital asking for an itemised statement of the treatment for Bobbie that I had been charged for. It seemed such an exorbitant amount to me and a reasonable request under the circumstances. $4650 and no statement of the cost!

I gave them what I thought was a reasonable time to reply, two weeks, and sent the letter I had written off to them. They had not replied after about six weeks, so

I wrote again asking that they respond in two weeks' time. By the end of that I still had not heard so I rang the ombudsman office and discussed it with them. They were very helpful and supportive.

As part of their support they also followed up by contacting the veterinary hospital, but they did not receive a response in the time requested either. However, I think they did a few days later, and this letter was to offer me something like a 10% refund!

Well!! You know what they could do with that!

With my blood well and truly up, I definitely was not happy with that so I went to the Australian Competition and Consumer Commission (ACCC) to take it to mediation and arbitration. At the ACCC there is a "hearing" with both parties present and then you are directed to go to a room and negotiate a decision. There was a man there representing the veterinary hospital I thought looked pretty uncomfortable, so I felt emboldened by that. I was determined to get some reasonable refund because the list of treatments was obviously so overdone. They appeared to be billing for treatments they were unsure had ever been completed! Even though they were the "specialist small animals' hospital," they did not find a tick until more than twelve hours after the dog was admitted, and still the poor dog died!

Anyway, the vet representative tried to defend the billing and then I just got stuck into him, remarkably calmly I thought at the time, about overcharging. The dog obviously had a tick, yet they did not find it until much later. Despite the huge list of individually charged interventions and treatments, he still died. And then they had the effrontery of charging more than $4500 payable before they would release the body. He knew I was furious but at the same time I was quite composed and assertive. I was proud of myself.

He then asked what I would be happy with. I had intended to ask for 50% of the cost as a refund, but I thought, "What the hell, I'll go for 75%." He so readily agreed that I was annoyed I hadn't demanded more! He still retained over $1200 for what was very unprofessional treatment; he got off very lightly.

Overall, I was proud to have been determined and assertive in this matter. It helped me gain the confidence that I could be again in the future.

Chapter Fifty-Two

Exhibiting in London

I had secured a small studio at the Lennox Street Studios, an old schoolhouse building full of about thirty-four artists, a few years before. As time passed and they became available I was able to gradually move to larger spaces that had more light. Wherever I was in the building I loved having that space to work in, and my painting slowly evolved. Eventually I secured a top floor studio with great light. I loved that space and spent many happy hours there.

My painting had been progressing well for a number of years. I tried to get there as much as I could but often weeks would pass before I could get to it for a few hours at least. With all of what was happening for me over those years that's what I tried for; a few hours at a time.

I had been like that with the pottery, too, not doing anything for weeks or months sometimes, then entering into a constant stream of productive work. I managed to sell my art occasionally and the recognition, appreciation and feedback — not the money so much — was rewarding. I justified the rent of the space as my reward, my space for just me to enjoy. I did some good work in those years and loved displaying it in the studio.

I did well with the painting at times and sold a number of works, especially at the annual exhibition and sale. I entered a work on two different occasions, one in the Wynne Prize for landscape and another, a portrait of Peter Rushforth in the Archibald, both at the New South Wales Art Gallery. Neither were successful in being chosen but my goal was to get a work done to a satisfactory standard that I felt good about entering the competition. I was successful at achieving that with those two paintings.

The main lessee of the Lennox Street Studios building had friends in London and knew the art world there a little. He had been invited to present an exhibition at the Menier Chocolate Factory Gallery in Southwark near the Tate Modern Gallery. A couple of other artists from the Studios were invited to exhibit as well and all reports said it was a rewarding experience.

The Royal Academy in London was planning a large Australian Landscape retrospective for exhibition in September 2013. The Menier Gallery invited Lennox Street Studios to mount an exhibition of Contemporary Australian Landscape painters to provide current work to appear in conjunction with the retrospective. I jumped at the chance to be one of the exhibitors, even though it would cost me an arm and a leg in time and money.

Eight of us were asked to present a unique interpretation of contemporary Australian landscape painting. We had been planning for about a year, and I was committed emotionally and financially to making it a success. This was a big event for me.

I planned to get the paintings stretched in London but that was going to cost a fortune. Instead I had them stretched in Sydney and then I packed them and air freighted the lot over in one large box — what an effort! I was lucky to have Maz, Ed's daughter, working there — in Threadneedle Street no less — such a romantic Shakespearean sounding name! Both Maz and her employers were very generous in allowing me to have the paintings delivered to their office. They allowed me to store them there and use the office facilities for last minute paperwork, signs and organising. I was very grateful to all of them. They also allowed me to leave the paintings there at the conclusion of the exhibition and have them collected to freight back to Australia. Having the paintings delivered to Maz's office in central London made things a lot easier.

From there I carried them to the Menier Gallery in Southwark by taxi. The exhibiting artists set up the exhibition and here we were, exhibiting internationally!

Chapter Fifty-Three

Coming to a Head

My relationship with Ed had been deteriorating rapidly for a considerable amount of time, and I was past making the effort to keep us afloat. I had been paying both shares of the mortgage for some time, Ed only occasionally having the funds to cover his share. I had been paying for the extensive renovations that we had been doing. I had paid a large proportion of the trip to Vietnam we shared earlier that year. I was doing these things because I felt deep compassion for him. I knew he was suffering from depression and that he was unhappy with how his family was treating him. I clung to the hope that all my emotional and financial support might assist him to get through this arduous and demeaning struggle for settlement with his ex and recover from his depression. I wanted him to start settling into some regular work and pulling his weight financially.

From my perspective, how I felt and the circumstances of our relationship made it patently obvious that my efforts had little effect. The constant effort on my part to keep working two careers, in school and in private practice and to have the funds to meet expenses was exhausting me. Trying to find time to paint and to support Ed through all this was draining my energy and my spirit. I ran out of patience and energy for the relationship. Even though I still loved Ed, I was angry and frustrated at his inability to get his act together and earn enough to pay his part of the deal financially. I was angry at his seeming inability to settle into and complete work on time and get paid for it. Angry at his distraction and behaviour with the dogs and frustrated and angry at what all this continued to mean for me. On the other hand, there was this conflict. In my more reflective moments I knew he was, and he still is, a loving and compassionate man.

All this came to a head while I was in London. The story with Ed would always be the same. He rarely had the money to pay his share of the mortgage. He kept getting me to cover for him and said he would pay me back, which rarely happened. I kept telling myself that things would get better and he would start to meet his obligations and responsibilities, but it never happened. I knew he was depressed, that he suffered from anxiety. But I was angry and trapped. I loved him despite all that.

The months before I was to leave for London, I kept reminding him that I was relying on him. I wanted and expected him to meet his mortgage payment for that month as I didn't have ready access to any more money to cover for him, and it was too difficult to arrange to cover his share at short notice from a distance. I also had a fear of defaulting on our mortgage again. The bank had been very difficult to deal with after the first incident, and I did not want to have to deal with it again. No matter what, I always had the mortgage covered each month, with Ed's support or not. Perhaps he knew that whether he came good with his share or not I would always cover it.

The day the mortgage was due to come out of our account, Ed hadn't paid his share. I then received an email from him, as I had before on numerous occasions, saying that he was hard up for cash and could I cover him for this month and he would pay me back. The same old story again!

After my emphasising to him that I needed him to cover his share this month and why, I felt furious and let down and frustrated with him. I sent him a pretty angry email about how I felt, then I found the money to cover the mortgage, and went off to my planned exploration of Turkey. I didn't hear a peep from Ed after his email and after I had had a go at him. I began to worry that he had retreated into himself again, vulnerable, hurt and wounded as he had in the past.

Chapter Fifty-Four

Surprise Berlin Vacation

My friend Don had heard that I was going to London, and he told me he would be there at the same time. He was visiting his sister in Hamburg beforehand and staying in Berlin for a week after that. He asked if I would be interested in joining him. A second visit to Berlin was certainly on my bucket list even after forty years. However, I had planned to be in London that week organising the paintings so hadn't given it much thought. Since I had already had the canvases stretched it meant that I didn't need to be there, so I was free to take up Don's suggestion I join him for a week in Berlin.

I rang him and said that my plans had changed, and I could get to Berlin on the week he was to be there. He organised a hotel room and we were to meet on the Thursday. What I hadn't realised was that Don was planning to be in Berlin because it was the week of Berlin "Folsom," a week of parties and clubs to celebrate Berlin Gay Leather. What a gift! A week of gay men in leather and parties and clubs in Berlin as an add-on to my break overseas. I had stayed with other gay friends in the same hotel bed in a non-sexual way and didn't give it any thought that I would be sharing a bed with Don though my hopes were aroused that it would be different.

I had been attracted to Don since meeting him at one of his dinner parties many years before. I'd see him at the Phoenix occasionally and have a little flirt with him, but he always shrugged me off because, as he told me later, I was in a relationship. I was — but hey, nothing wrong with a little flirting with an attractive man! So, a leather week with him in Berlin was a bonus. I have always liked men in leather and a whole week of Berlin with men in leather sounded very appealing!! I had actually brought some smaller leather accessories with me to wear to London parties so it was lucky I had some with me.

I met Don at the hotel on Thursday evening and we went out for a meal and a few beers at a local club and then home. As Don was getting ready to retire, I was laying on the bed feeling cheeky. He began putting pyjama pants on.

I said, "What are you putting those on for?"

"Because I'm getting ready for bed," he said.

"Get them off or I'll rip the bloody things off you," I said.

He needed no more encouragement and dropped them on the floor and got into bed. The rest is history. We began a relationship from then on.

In my mind it was an opportunity too good to pass up. Here I was, on holiday, in Berlin, about to have a week of bars and parties in such a sexy city, with a good-looking man for company. This was a holiday fling; lots of people have holiday flings, don't they? I was determined I would enjoy it for the week and then return to my normal life with Ed in Sydney, leaving any affair behind.

As mentioned, things had not been too good between Ed and I for some time, especially from my perspective. I was getting frustrated and disappointed at where our relationship was going, and what it was meaning for me. Berlin offered a chance to escape that with a good friend to share it with. And we did have a good time; at parties like "Pig" and another one in an abandoned industrial site, in clubs and cellars, the daytime leather fair, and the sights of Berlin "being out there!" And Berlin was "out there!" They are very open about their sexual behaviour, and many times I was gobsmacked by what was happening right in front of my eyes. I loved that week; it was great, completely unexpected and a very liberating experience.

Then it was over, and London called. Don came back to London for the week of the exhibition and rented a room in Soho, so I spent some nights at Maz's and some nights at his place. I would guess that Maz deduced what was happening though not a word was said.

The week of the exhibition was interesting and busy. The eight of us mounted a very impressive exhibition of our work. It was opened by the High Commissioner of London at the time, Mike Rann, formerly the Labour Premier of South Australia. Everyone sold at least something, including me, so it wasn't a financial disaster. It was fun taking my turn at fronting the gallery, talking to people about art, Australia, and London, and making the occasional sale for others or myself.

It was a lot of work to organise and cost a bundle, but I am very satisfied to know that my art was part of an exhibition in London. It looks good on my Artist CV!

The week passed quickly. Don and I went out to get some London gay night life and see exhibitions and a musical. London is such a great city and I feel at home there, confident in knowing my way around.

Soon it was time to dismantle the exhibition, send it off to Sydney, and embark on the next part of my holiday before heading home to Sydney and Ed. Sixteen days in Turkey; a place I had never been before.

Don departed for Sydney and me for Istanbul. As far as I was concerned that was the end of the affair with Don. I was looking forward to a holiday in Turkey although at the time not relishing going home to Ed.

Chapter Fifty-Five

Cappadocia Carnival

About a week passed with me doing a tour of the ancient archaeological cities of eastern Turkey and a tour of Gallipoli. I was never keen to visit Gallipoli, as I have not been with other war action sites. However, I found it quietly dignified and honouring of both Australia's contribution and that of the opposing Turks. I was quietly impressed by it, much to my surprise.

After the week of touring fascinating ancient sites, I arrived in Cappadocia. The next morning, I was booked to do a dawn balloon flight over the spires of Cappadocia and the following morning return to Istanbul. Eighty-three balloons airborne at once in the dawn light was quite spectacular! I had never done a balloon flight before and this was special. It was a remarkable finish to my week of touring Turkey.

I began to get urgent messages from Robert, Ed's son in Sydney, and Maz in London indicating Ed was seriously ill in hospital. They said he could die, and I had better get home as soon as possible. I was so confused, upset, and worried about what I might have contributed to this crisis. I was then panicked about how I was going to manage to get home as quickly as possible. I was in a dusty bus park at a carpet factory, walking distractedly around in circles, frantic and in tears, talking to Maz. As the tour was ending, I had a booked flight to Istanbul the next day, so that part was okay. I'd get back to Istanbul and find a flight home from there.

Getting home in an emergency is such a stressful and unexpected trial. I'd heard about the difficulty of dealing with airlines that are overbooked and not interested in your plight, trying to deal with airline staff, trying to find a spare seat — and book it! At least I had travel insurance and reasoned that should pay for the expense of a new ticket. In an emergency you can't buy on a discount or a travel deal.

That night I was booked into a "cave accommodation" in Cappadocia. There was little internet reception, so I spent the night trying to navigate the web and find the quickest flight path back to Sydney. I tried to get something through the Middle East like with Etihad but to no avail. I tried to find a flight direct to Sydney from Istanbul, but they don't seem to exist, especially at short notice. I felt like I was in a daze trying to deal with what might be happening for Ed, what might be happening in Sydney, what might be my role in all this, and what I had been up to with Don. Little did I know what stress was!

I decided that next morning I would use the booked flight I already had back to Istanbul and book a flight back to London that day, reasoning that at least I would be able to organise something in an English language country and in a city I was familiar with. I contacted Maz and booked a flight to London. Maz had already booked a flight from London back to Sydney leaving that night, but she had managed to locate a seat on a Cathay Pacific flight leaving the next morning that was being held for me for twelve hours until I got to London and could book it there. Some (temporary) relief and a possible solution!

I flew back to Istanbul the next morning, but timing meant that I didn't have time to get into the centre of the city and get the carpets I had bought earlier. I had done so with the plan of shipping them back to Sydney in my luggage. I had purposely paid for a premium economy fare so I could have additional baggage weight allowance. However, that plan had to be abandoned because my flight to London departed almost immediately and left me no time to collect the carpets in the city.

By the time I got to Heathrow I urgently needed to get to a computer so I could book the ticket on the Sydney flight that was being held for me. Maz had given me the details so after clearing customs, with great relief I found some computers available to the public in the terminal.

Chapter Fifty-Six

Aren't We Thankful for Technology?

Would you believe the keyboard of the computer I was paying for at Heathrow was faulty! I had to keep putting £2 coins into it to keep it functioning, and several times I ran out of coins so had to start again. As part of the process I had to fill out an online form and the keys kept getting stuck so I would end up with a line of eeeeeeeeeeeeeeee's or mmmmmmmmmmmmmmmm's!

Eventually I was able to speak to the travel clerk holding the booking and he asked me if I was using a credit card issued in London as the system would only accept that. OMG! Can you imagine the state of stress I was in? Of course, my credit card wasn't issued in London, but it was nevertheless a perfectly good credit card issued in Sydney! So why wouldn't it accept that?!

After quite a while of this stress and frustration — the level of which I never want to experience again — he agreed with me and booked the seat. This meant I was flying out the next morning with a stopover in Hong Kong airport. But at least I was on my way to Sydney. I stayed the night at Maz's flat and got to Heathrow nice and early the next day.

The flight to Sydney via Hong Kong with Cathay Pacific was one of the best I have had. I had no idea what I was flying home to find, nor how I would deal with the turmoil that was waiting for me. I used the time to practice calming myself and readying myself for the drama I was to enter.

It was late Saturday night when I landed at Sydney. My son, Lenny, met me at Arrivals, and we drove direct to St. Vincent's Hospital to see Ed.

I had heard from phone conversations with Robert and Maz that he was in a very bad way and perhaps not expected to live, but what I saw was totally shocking.

Ed was huddled on the Intensive Care bed, thin as a rake, and mottled black and blue over his entire body. He was barely conscious. The doctors explained that he was close to death when he was admitted on the Wednesday. He had begun to respond to drugs, but they thought he would still lose his legs, his arms and perhaps his nose and ears. They reported that his entire body, including his testicles, were black and mottled. His body had been completely shutting down and gone into toxic shock. He had been found just in time. However, their prognosis was not positive and he would be lucky to survive. I remember thinking, "Ed, if you lose your limbs you would be better off dead." But, amazingly, he was staying alive and his condition slowly improved.

I gathered some of the story later from Jeff, the good friend of ours who had found him. Apparently, on his birthday about four days after the mortgage was due to be paid, he bought another dog from the doggie rescue. A birthday present to himself. Ed had had the money for another dog but not the mortgage! He knew my views about a third dog in the house. He would have played and roistered with them in the house. The other dogs were used to his playing antics and wouldn't have reacted, but this dog was new and did not have that experience.

Apparently, it reacted to his roughhouse play and bit him on the hand. Ed didn't treat the wound properly and left it there. That weekend he went to a dance party with some friends, he would have had a good time as we liked to do, came home sometime Sunday morning and crashed on the couch in the kitchen with the dogs. Jeff received a call from Ed on Tuesday evening asking him to take him to the doctor as he thought he had an attack of shingles. Jeff's response was that he didn't sound too bad, and besides the doctors would all be closed at that hour; he would call around at lunchtime tomorrow to see how he was, to which Ed agreed.

By the time Jeff got there at lunchtime Wednesday and finally got Ed to open the door, he was appalled at what he saw. Ed insisted he be taken to his GP in Lane Cove, not straight to Emergency as Jeff wanted. When they got there the response was the same: take him immediately to Emergency at North Shore Hospital.

Ed wanted to go to St. Vincent's Hospital, so they went there and, as Jeff reports, as soon as they saw the state Ed was in it was all systems alert. Ed was rushed into Emergency and admitted to the Intensive Care Unit (ICU). It had been about six or seven days since he had been bitten by the dog. He must have been in a dreadful state. When Hugo found out, he went to the house and cleaned up the mess that Ed had left, especially in the kitchen and the sofa. Ed must have been very ill during this time.

The doctors said he had contracted a bacterial infection from the dog's saliva and that this had attacked his body. His body had gone into toxic shock and was shutting down. By the time he got to hospital, his kidneys, liver and so on were dysfunctional; his entire body was in shut down. His chances of survival were slim, and even if he did survive, he would lose much of his body: arms, legs, facial features and so on due to the infection.

During the next six weeks, Ed would lose both his legs from below the knee, requiring him to manage life on prosthetics.

The sight was horrific. Mottled skin over fleshless bones. Amazingly, he responded to treatment and began to become conscious, although still very ill and bedridden. That's where I saw him, by then after midnight the next day. By this stage it was nine days after the dog bite and three days since he had been admitted to hospital.

So now I was back in Sydney, my partner Ed in intensive care, I was back at work trying to earn some money to stay afloat. What to do about Ed? What to do about Don? I would get to work in the morning, close the office door, put my head down and howl out my anxiety and grief into tissues and the waste bin.

As a side note, I made a claim with the travel insurance company later (following the success of the claim for the dog's veterinary expenses through the ACCC) for a refund of the plane tickets to return to Australia. It was also for the cost of the carpets that I didn't have time to get from the dealer in Istanbul to fly them by post to Australia, but no luck. I know the conditions of the travel insurance precluded a claim for carpets, but my argument was that this expense would not have occurred if it wasn't for the fact that I had to return to Australia urgently and would not have incurred this expense if the trip had been as planned. But no luck.

Why else do we pay for travel insurance if it is not to claim on legitimate and unforeseen expenses? They stuck by their conditions as I knew they would. Worth a try though. They did give me $250 as compensation! Conscience money.

Chapter Fifty-Seven

The Way Life Is

Don kept me sane during this stressful time. His apartment was only about a ten-minute walk from St. Vincent's so I would go to work from his place. After work, I went to the hospital and dealt with what was needed about the house, money, debt, trying to plan what needed to be done. Then I'd go home to Don's place and he would cook dinner and we'd relax and go to bed. He was quietly strong and supportive. It's what I needed at the time.

I was in a quandary as I hadn't told Ed about Don and needed to do it. My feelings for Ed despite my frustrations, impatience and disappointment with him and how he'd got into this mess were still there. Here I was, having an affair with someone he knew while he was barely surviving in Intensive Care. What did this say about me? I was deserting him, leaving him to his fate. I felt such intense shame. This was not how I wanted to behave, yet I knew that I couldn't stay with Ed either. My resentment and frustrations with him would soon resurface and poison our relationship. A huge decision and not an honourable one from any perspective, whether I chose to leave Ed and abandon him, or stay with him and deal with the consequences.

Neither option was the most positive and best one. It has left me feeling challenged and disappointed.

Our friends also knew I was living with Don and that Ed still thought he and I were an item. When I told Ed I was having an affair with Don, he crumbled. He was, understandably, desperate in his reactions and attempts to get me to change my mind and agree to stay. He begged me to not leave him, that he loved me, he wanted to stay with me. My heart went out to him, but I knew I had to remain resolute. I had to be really determined that I would not give into him. Much as I knew it broke his heart, I also knew I could not stay with him. I had to be a bastard and harden myself to him.

By this time, I was living with Don; at least with him I didn't feel like I was breaking all the time. I knew I would resent Ed intensely if I felt trapped into living with him after this. Ed had weeks and weeks in Intensive Care and then in rehabilitation at St. Vincent's. He made remarkable progress in dealing with the loss of his feet and legs, in learning to navigate and propel himself in his wheelchair, and then in learning to walk on his prosthetic feet and legs. He was very determined. Occasionally his family would come to see him. Ed's older sister, Clare, saw him a couple of times and was obviously emotionally affected by his condition. Her son, Ed's nephew, also came and was very solicitous for his welfare. I knew from Ed that the family were comfortably off.

All this time I was beside myself with anxiety about the whole situation. I had a couple of conversations with Clare about Ed, and she insisted that she be kept informed of any developments in his condition. On a subsequent phone call, I let my guard down and told her how desperate I was feeling about Ed and the financial situation we were in. At this time she insisted to me that I write her a letter, stating emphatically "and give me the facts." She said that a couple of times so, feeling

I needed some understanding and support, I thought "Okay, I'll give you the facts." I was feeling very low and despondent about the whole situation. In a rush of stupidity, I wrote her a letter setting out the sordid mess of our financial affairs.

A few days later I received a call from Ed's nephew accusing me of worrying his "aged mother," and "how dare I involve [his] mother in my financial matters, that these were for Ed and me to work out not his mother." There was a considerable amount of bullying language in this vein. I was very angry that he responded in this unfair way. At the time I simply could not be bothered trying to explain to him why I had written the letter and that his "aged mother" had requested I write and give her "the facts." I know I should have responded to him, but I didn't have it in me. Another case of bullying males. I don't think I felt as traumatised by his arrogance and language as I had in the past, just angry that he had the arrogance and insensitivity to do it. And it made me feel more despondent about our situation; about carrying the load myself.

Sometime after this Ed eventually came back to live with me in Newtown. We shared the house and I was his carer. I drove him to medical and other appointments and cooked and kept house, but as time went on I remained determined to go through with the separation even though I knew Ed was in such anguish about my leaving him. I knew that if I stayed with Ed, I would regret it and resent being trapped. I did not want this.

When it was obvious to Ed that we were not going to have a reconciliation he eventually agreed to put the Newtown house on the market. It sold at auction for a good price for the day. Similar to the Darlington house, I regret selling the Newtown house because it was a solid investment and had great potential. At least the new owners had the finances to capitalise on it when, unfortunately, we didn't.

I needed to be away from Ed and his reliance on me. After selling the Newtown house I took my share to buy a small flat of my own. I bought in the Inner West and spent a lot of my savings on renovations as I wanted it to be a good place to live in; to be my place. It looked great when the renovations were done but by then I had moved in permanently with Don, so I rented the flat out to pay the mortgage. It's still there if I ever need it. Maybe I will have my own place to live in at the end of my story. Maybe I won't. That's the way life is.

Chapter Fifty-Eight

Up Muddy Mountain Tracks on a Pony

Bhutan was on my bucket list. Friends of mine were there doing a volunteer/exchange stint in the capital Thimbu and invited me over if I wanted to come. I went.

What a fascinating country. It cost a lot to get the visa but then the cost covered most of the accommodation, a guide, a trek and other expenses. We went trekking up a steep mountain near the capital. My left knee, which for a long time had been painful, collapsed completely. It had been playing up for years and I had been nursing it along, but this really wrecked it. I also had a lot of nausea from the altitude so the whole holiday wasn't the greatest of success stories. I spent most of the trek clutching on to a pony that scrambled up and down these incredible tracks. But Bhutan itself was a fascinating country with beautiful, proud and dignified people and spectacular mountains. I was happy to get home eventually and then within weeks had my knee replaced. An expensive operation but the relief was immediate.

I've had still no luck with the tinnitus in my head. I will have to learn to cope with it. Tinnitus is one of those bloody ailments that simply will not ever go away yet has such an effect on every waking and sleeping moment. Always carrying this distracting and disabling noise everywhere, every waking moment. It affects everything. It's there now – a huge dominating buzzing in my head.

At the end of 2018 I had to go to see my neurosurgeon at Royal Prince Alfred Hospital in Sydney as I was having more headaches, nausea and unsteadiness. She said I should have the shunt re-inserted to drain off the excess fluid, a build-up of hydrocephaly. I was admitted to hospital several times over summer as they adjusted the shunt and attempted to use different approaches to alleviate the problem. At the end of a consultation in January 2019, I was immediately readmitted to hospital for emergency surgery. I found out later that I had contracted a golden staph infection, I assumed from one of the previous hospital admissions. It appears that I was not expected to live through that as it was in my brain and difficult to treat. This required a lengthy stay of six weeks in Intensive Care and a longer time on antibiotic infusions after my discharge. But I survived. I'm still here. It's weird to think I was almost dead, almost no longer here!

Chapter Fifty-Nine

Tripping

The doctors told my sons I had a golden staph infection and that I might die, so they should see me soon. As I mentioned, I must have picked it up when I had the operations on my brain to insert and alter the shunts. This infection could easily kill me.

While in Intensive Care I was unconscious and semi-conscious and on lots of drugs. Weird things were happening. I'm losing my stuff, my wallet, my phone. My cards, my watch. All gone. I can't find them again. Has someone taken them? They must be here somewhere. Lost. All the stuff we need for everyday living. What is going on? I'm confused. They say I can't drive anymore. They've stopped my licence. They've stolen my independence. I'll have to rely on others to drive me around. I hate relying on others. I hate being dependent.

Seems my sight is playing up. Seeing double now: I'm cross-eyed. I can't read anymore. The CT scans have stuffed my visual nerves; frazzled them; fried them. The photos of my eyes look hideous. Printing has become muddled. Lines of print are off balance. If I cover one eye it's sort of OK but the print lines run into and over each other and making sense of printing and reading becomes impossible.

Sound is weird, confused, jumbled, repetitive. Seems I am in Intensive Care, I recognise that. I'm in the centre of the ward. Everybody checks on me. Seems like everything is constantly changing. I'm on a changing film set. People coming and going, doing tests on me, taking blood. Now we're in another country. Sometimes there is the same doctor, but the film set had changed.

Nobody explains. How come nobody explains? Would I understand? What is going on?

The set seems to change all the time. Each time I wake up there are different people, coming and going, coming and going. Talking to me, doing things to me. Are we in a different country? We seem to be. Have they moved me to a hospital in a different place? Maybe I'm in Western Australia? In southern California? The people seem different. Different people. Maybe they've moved me to New York? To a new place somewhere, for more up to date care?

Maybe I am really ill? But this doesn't matter as I am happy to be on these drugs, to be in a new place.

The strings of sounds play over and over. Repetitive music. I like it. I'd like to tape the music. It's very relaxing and meditative. Some is like rap; some is like hallucinatory sounds and music. Over and over the repetitive sounds are running into each other, like drugs, like being stoned and floating. Beep, beep, beep. The lights of the images emerging into my consciousness are muted and comforting colours: yellows, lemons, whites and blues, hues and shades, lavenders, pulsating and swelling, like waves of colour and sound weaving in and out of my consciousness. Like being stoned and snuggled comfortably in a beach humpy, the ebb and swell of waves, the ebb and swell of sounds, the flow and rhythm of the colours and the images and the sounds. Snuggled, warm and comforted by the music, the colours and smells in a beach humpy. Warm and protected.

My son comes to see me.

"The doctors are worried about you, Dad. They say you might die. That this might do you in."

Die? Am I dying? Is this what it's like to die? I don't want to die just yet. I'm only seventy-one. I've still got a lot of things to do. I'm too young to die. I like the hallucinating. I like the soft music and colours of the beach humpy. But I don't want to die. A bit longer.

My sister rings. I tell her I am hallucinating; that they're feeding me hallucinatory drugs. She thinks this is a great joke. She says she'll write about this on Facebook. I worry that someone will find out about it and the hospital will get into trouble. The old paranoia returns. I tell my sister this and she laughs. This is the drugs and the infection having an effect on your brain, she says.

Sometimes I wake up and Don is here, then he's gone. Or my friends come and go. Or my sons. It is good to wake and see them but then the next time they aren't there.

I learn that I am getting large infusions of antibiotics, which cause the hallucinating. I just need to relax and enjoy the drugs. I can relax and enjoy it. The sounds, the meditative music. The images of the hippy beach humpy, the colours return. The people change, the film set changes again, the people change. I am again in a new film set, the people are making a film about me and how they are treating my brain infection.

At least my headaches have eased, have gone in fact. No more constant headaches. And the nausea has gone too, no more feeling like I am going to throw up. No starting to cough that leads into retching and throwing up.

But my eyesight is wrecked. I am seeing double all the time. I look at something square — a door, a cupboard — and the lines intersect. I look at the nurse's station where the nurses and doctors are just beyond the end of my bed. They are all out of focus and multiple images. They talk. It's all garbled. There are multiples of them, everything is blurred. Reading is impossible, the lines intersperse and overlap. The words are superimposed. I can't read my novel for book club; it is so difficult. I can't do it. Impossible. It takes such a long time. I have to have a patch over one eye.

My sons appear. They have come to visit me; it is so good to see them. But how did they get here? Are we in southern California? I worry that it has cost them a lot of money to get here from Australia. They seem unconcerned at my worry for them and they laugh off my anxiety, which doesn't help. Why are they laughing?

My brain is wondering about what is happening. I have to tell myself that I am being looked after and that I will be okay. But it's weird — how can I be okay when I feel like I am being filmed, that I am in a film set, that I am snuggled up in a beach humpy, with sounds, music, repetitive images, stoned, colours, billowing sheets that seem like filmy sarongs, people, being moved, moving me around. Jabbing me with needles. The music continues, repetitive, it is the monitors and the instruments. The set has changed again.

I could die here. Maybe this means I am dying. But I don't want to die yet. I am too young. What about my kids, my grandkids? I won't get to see them anymore, nor will they see me. I need to live more years, there is still too much to do. I don't want it to end yet. I want to swim in the ocean again. To feel what it's like. The cool water. Though I could die, it could end. It might be easier. It might mean that I don't have to struggle anymore. I don't have to worry about life anymore. But no, I am too young to die, it is too early for me, there is still more to do. More things I want to do.

The neurosurgeon called around to see me and said they had expected to lose me during the night. I knew I had been very ill but by that time was feeling a little more alive. I thought to myself then that I want to live until I'm eighty.

From then on, I recovered well and after weeks of daily antibiotic infusions I was taken off antibiotics and am now, with rest and exercise, becoming healthier every day. My eyesight, which was fried by the number of CT scans I had, is taking a long time and much expense to get better. It's not there yet.

It appears that I am clear of the infection now; at least I hope I am. The neurosurgeon told me they were afraid that they would lose me but happy to see me recover of course! So am I. My sons, who were told I may not survive, are happy also.

So, I didn't die. I have decided to live some more. So, what it takes now is to get better. Not just at surviving, but at living. The way life is.

Chapter Sixty

The Way Life Is Now

What now then? I just celebrated my seventy-second birthday with my children, grandchildren, and with my partner, Don, all beautiful people. Don and I went to New York to celebrate my birthday. I love New York, the people, the bustle, the art galleries. Actually, I got approached by a NY gallery to see if I wanted to join their "stable." I checked it out when I was there and wasn't overly impressed; and it would have cost a bomb. It's obviously a marketing strategy for them. That means no art for me in New York.

I walked the High Line twice and loved it. It is an innovative piece of social infrastructure. The buildings and streets, the buzz and bustle. Spent fifteen days walking around the East Village. Poking into galleries, hanging out, beers and tacos in the local bar, the 9/11 Memorial, so dignified and impressive. Saw a performance of the Warsaw Symphony Orchestra in the Lincoln Centre. What a buzz. Three days in Chicago; such a different city to New York. Then back to Long Island for another three days to say farewell. I love New York. I could live there. But maybe only for a few months. I think it might overwhelm me if I stayed too long.

The last week in Sydney I did a senior's jazz and tap dance class at Sydney Dance Company. Loved it.

Writers group, book club, yoga in the morning, tri-weekly bike riding for exercise.

Now I'm well into my 70's — older than Mum was when she died. Alice and I just drove across the Nullarbor Plain, the width of Australia, in her campervan. A long trip but so glad we did it. What a fun challenge.

My head almost finished me off earlier this year but now I'm still alive! Still recovering, still exercising, regular yoga in the mornings. I had a run on the beach this morning. Then a swim in the ocean, so cool and refreshing. I had a coffee overlooking the waves and the surfers. Doing regular long rides on my bike. Breakfast on the back deck looking into the rain forest. Some painting. Reading books for my two book clubs, the Sydney one and the Port one.

This is my life, why I'm here now. Living with Don and our dog, Maxie. This is the way life is. For now.

About the Author

Tony now lives with his partner, Don, on the Mid North Coast of NSW. Now retired he loves riding his bicycle, swimming in the ocean, keeping fit with yoga, writing and not often enough meditating. He has been a potter in the past and occasionally paints with acrylics.

He has work in collections in Great Britain, the USA and Australia. Tony has lived in the Blue Mountains and the Inner West of Sydney and grew up on the edge of the wilds of the Colo region northwest of Sydney.

Tony has been a teacher and school counsellor and has had a private psychology counselling practice for the past twenty years. He started a journal about fifteen years ago and this book has grown out of that. Writing has been a big part of his professional life, but this is the first time he has published writing.

Tony has two wonderful adult sons and two beautiful grandchildren. This book is for them.

Acknowledgements

What a rewarding and challenging experience it has been writing this book and getting it to a stage where I felt it was worthwhile publishing and "putting myself out there in front of everyone." My grateful thanks to the staff at Tellwell Publishing, especially Redjell, my co-ordinator; and to Darin, my editor, for his editing, his insights, his empathy, and his interest in Australia!

Sharing my writing and progress with the U3A Port Macquarie Writers, Group has been very helpful. I want to thank my good friend, Dr. Barbara Bee, for her critical, supportive and honest insights and suggestions. Also my good friend Philip Ritchie for sharing his design knowledge.

Front cover painting "Sentinels," acrylic on canvas, by Tony Williams.

I also want to thank all those people who might find themselves mentioned in the book; they helped my life to be "less ordinary" and *The Way Life Is*.

Lightning Source UK Ltd.
Milton Keynes UK
UKHW012028300720
367452UK00005BA/139